NORTH AMERICAN WILDLIFE
BIRDS

READER'S DIGEST
NORTH AMERICAN

WILDLIFE

BIRDS

The Reader's Digest Association, Inc.
Pleasantville, New York/Montreal

A READER'S DIGEST BOOK

Edited and designed by Media Projects Incorporated

Editors:
Edward S. Barnard
Sharon Fass Yates

Managing Editor:
Lelia Mander

Assistant Editor:
Aaron Murray

Production Manager:
Laura Smyth

Design:
Design Oasis

Copy Editor:
Charlotte Maurer

Consultant for revised edition:
Robert E. Budliger
Dir. of Environmental
Education (retired)
NY State Department of
Environmental Conservation

The credits and acknowledgments that appear on page 216 are hereby made a part of this copyright page.

Library of Congress Cataloging in Publication Data
Birds.
    p. cm. (North American Wildlife)
    Includes Index.
    ISBN 0-7621-0036-2
    1. Birds—North America—Identification. I. Reader's Digest
    Association.
QL681.N67   1998
598'.097—dc21   97-32723

This book contains revised material originally published in 1982 in the Reader's Digest book, NORTH AMERICAN WILDLIFE.

Printed in the United States of America
Second Printing, April 2000

CONTENTS

ABOUT THIS BOOK

More than any other form of wildlife, birds hold us happily captive in their spell. They are active and attractive. They make beautiful music. They please us with their willingness to come to feeders, their preoccupation with nest and nestlings, their miraculous, mysterious ability to fly.

For some people, it is joy enough to see a bird and observe its actions. Others want to identify the bird, learn about its lifestyle and behavior. This book encourages both approaches to enjoying birds.

Part of our fascination with birds lies in their diversity and ubiquity. Upwards of 650 species are breeders or visitors north of the Mexican border. BIRDS doesn't attempt to show all of them. Instead, it concentrates on the ones people are most likely to see, our continent's more abundant or conspicuous species. It also illustrates some of the better known but rare birds such as the whooping crane.

To simplify recognition, swimming and wading birds have been separated from land birds. Within these two divisions, species are arranged in currently accepted scientific groupings, although the Starling, House Sparrow, and a few others are placed near species they resemble. Most species on facing pages are shown in scale with one another unless separated by a black line.

Where appropriate, the maps are subdivided to show separate breeding, wintering, and migration ranges. A word of caution, though: birds may stray from their usual range, and changes in ranges are

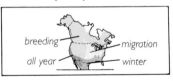

inevitable over time. The maps in this book are merely guides, not absolutes. Be delighted rather than dismayed should you find a bird in the "wrong" place or at the "wrong" time of year.

Many bird species have more than one distinctive plumage, and in many cases more than one form is illustrated in this book. For other species with major sexual or seasonal differences, the individual shown in the book is a male in breeding (summer) plumage unless otherwise noted.

HELPFUL IDENTIFICATION FEATURES

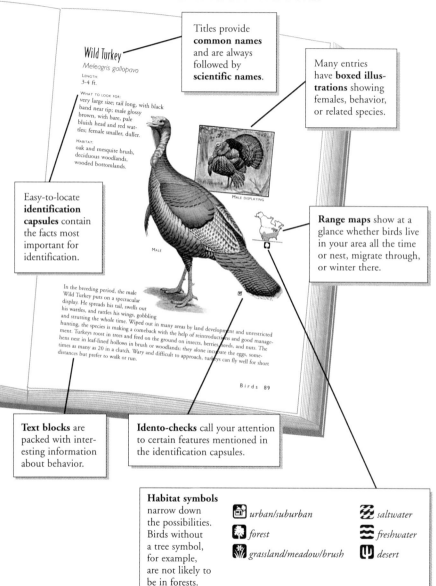

Titles provide **common names** and are always followed by **scientific names**.

Many entries have **boxed illustrations** showing females, behavior, or related species.

Easy-to-locate **identification capsules** contain the facts most important for identification.

Range maps show at a glance whether birds live in your area all the time or nest, migrate through, or winter there.

Text blocks are packed with interesting information about behavior.

Idento-checks call your attention to certain features mentioned in the identification capsules.

Habitat symbols narrow down the possibilities. Birds without a tree symbol, for example, are not likely to be in forests.

- urban/suburban
- forest
- grassland/meadow/brush
- saltwater
- freshwater
- desert

Wild Turkey
Meleagris gallopavo

LENGTH:
3–4 ft.

WHAT TO LOOK FOR:
very large size; tail long, with black band near tip; male glossy brown, with bare, pale bluish head and red wattles; female smaller, duller.

HABITAT:
oak and mesquite brush, deciduous woodlands, wooded bottomlands.

MALE DISPLAYING

MALE

In the breeding period, the male Wild Turkey puts on a spectacular display. He spreads his tail, swells out his wattles, and rattles his wings, gobbling and strutting the whole time. Wiped out in many areas by land development and unrestricted hunting, the species is making a comeback with the help of reintroductions and good management. Turkeys roost in trees and feed on the ground on insects, berries, seeds, and nuts. The hens nest in leaf-lined hollows in brush or woodlands; they alone incubate the eggs, sometimes as many as 20 in a clutch. Wary and difficult to approach, turkeys can fly well for short distances but prefer to walk or run.

Beginning or intermediate birders need little equipment. Most important is a pair of binoculars with central focusing and a seven- or eightfold magnification. Popular sizes for general use are 7 x 35 and 8 x 40. (The first number refers to magnification; the second, indirectly to light-gathering power.) Other aids you may want to carry along are a pocket-sized field guide and a notebook. Sooner or later, even casual bird-watchers start to keep records that, whether mere lists of species seen or more extensive notes, serve as a diary of birding experiences.

Many birders enjoy going out alone, and there is much to be said for a solitary early-morning walk or a restful hour near a pond or stream. But birding in a group that includes at least one experienced observer will speed up the learning process and furnish companionship and extra pairs of eyes as well. Many parts of the country have bird clubs that schedule meetings and outings where you can meet helpful birders. Try calling the biology department of a high school or college or the nearest natural history museum to find out about clubs and events in your area.

To maximize your opportunities to observe birds, keep in mind their flighty nature. Walk slowly and steadily, or not at all. (Birds are less skittish if you stay in the car.) Keep quiet. Don't wear bright clothing. And do get out early in the day, especially if you're looking for land birds in spring; they're most active from dawn to midmorning.

Don't be discouraged if you can't identify some of the birds you spot. A bird can be very hard to identify if it is immature or if it is molting its feathers, which all birds do at least once a year, usually in late summer or early fall. And remember that females are frequently quite different in color and markings from the males.

Orchard Oriole

In many species the most strikingly colored bird is the adult, breeding male. Young birds often look like the female.

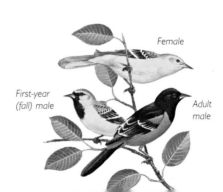

Female

First-year (fall) male

Adult male

TIPS FOR IDENTIFYING BIRDS

Posture and movement. The way a bird moves is a clue to its identity. Wrens cock their tails; woodpeckers have an undulating flight pattern. Check the species descriptions for such behavioral clues.

Color and markings. These attributes most tellingly reveal a bird's identity. In time, you will be able to take in more at a glance and concentrate on details separating closely related species—bill color on a tern, the presence or absence of wing bars on a vireo.

Size and proportions. Compare a bird you don't recognize with a Robin, crow, or other familiar species. Is it the same size? Is it streamlined or robust? How long or short are its legs and bill? Closely related species are pictured in scale, making differences obvious.

Songs and calls. It is often easier to recognize a bird by sound than by sight. Learn bird calls by listening to recordings or by spotting calling birds and identifying them. This book can only hint at the variety of bird vocalizations.

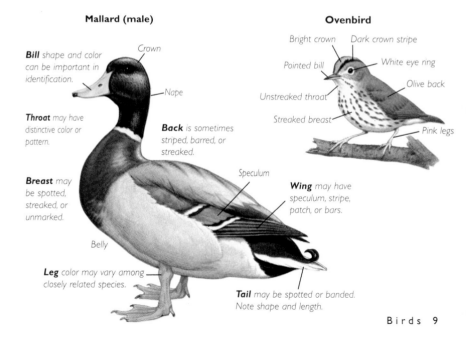

Mallard (male)

Bill shape and color can be important in identification.

Crown

Nape

Throat may have distinctive color or pattern.

Back is sometimes striped, barred, or streaked.

Breast may be spotted, streaked, or unmarked.

Speculum

Belly

Leg color may vary among closely related species.

Tail may be spotted or banded. Note shape and length.

Ovenbird

Bright crown   Dark crown stripe

Pointed bill

White eye ring

Olive back

Unstreaked throat

Streaked breast

Pink legs

Wing may have speculum, stripe, patch, or bars.

BIRDS WITH DISTINCTIVE TRAITS

To identify birds with a distinctive appearance or behavior, consult the lists that follow. The lists include only those species shown in this book, but the text accompanying an illustration may mention other species with similar traits. Because plumage may vary according to age, sex, season, and other factors, not all birds of a given species necessarily have the particular trait for which they are listed.

Rose, Red, or Orange
prominent color or markings

SMALL
Rufous
   Hummingbird p. 103
Vermilion
   Flycatcher p. 118
American Redstart p. 160
Blackburnian
   Warbler p. 173
Painted Bunting p. 189
Purple Finch p. 190
House Finch p. 191

Red Crossbill p. 190
Common Redpoll p. 192

MEDIUM
Red-bellied
   Woodpecker p. 106
Red-headed
   Woodpecker p. 106
Yellow-bellied
   Sapsucker p. 108
American Robin p. 146
Varied Thrush p. 147
Red-winged
   Blackbird p. 178
Scarlet Tanager p. 184

Western Tanager p. 185
Summer Tanager p. 184
Northern Cardinal p. 186
Rose-breasted
   Grosbeak p. 188
Black-headed
   Grosbeak p. 189
Pine Grosbeak p. 192

LARGE
Pileated
   Woodpecker p. 105

VERY LARGE
*Roseate Spoonbill p. 28

White
dominant color

SMALL
*Snowy Plover p. 50
Snow Bunting p. 208

MEDIUM
*Sanderling p. 57
*Least Tern p. 74

LARGE
*Snowy Egret p. 25
Cattle Egret p. 26
*Common
   Goldeneye p. 44
*Bufflehead p. 44
*Ring-billed Gull p. 67
*Bonaparte's Gull p. 70
*Forster's Tern p. 72
*Common Tern p. 72
*Caspian Tern p. 75
White-tailed
   Ptarmigan p. 86

VERY LARGE
*American White
   Pelican p. 19
*Northern Gannet p. 20
*Great Egret p. 25
*Wood Stork p. 29
*Whooping Crane p. 30
*Mute Swan p. 34
*Tundra Swan p. 35
*Snow Goose p. 36
*Herring Gull p. 67
Snowy Owl p. 95

associated mainly with water

Mostly Black

may show iridescence

SMALL
Chimney Swift p. 100
Lark Bunting p. 195

MEDIUM
* Leach's
   Storm-petrel p. 14
*Black Tern p. 74
 Purple Martin p. 128
 Phainopepla p. 152

Red-winged
   Blackbird p. 178
Brown-headed
   Cowbird p. 178
Brewer's Blackbird p. 181
European Starling p. 180

LARGE
*Common Gallinule p. 33
* American Coot p. 33
* Black Duck p. 39
* Black
   Oystercatcher p. 46

American Crow p. 125
Common
   Grackle p. 180

VERY LARGE
*Double-crested
   Cormorant p. 20
*Anhinga p. 21
*Glossy Ibis p. 26
 Turkey Vulture p. 78
 Common
   Raven p. 125

Bright Yellow

*prominent
color or markings*

SMALL
Verdin p. 130
Northern Parula p. 159
Prothonotary
   Warbler p. 160
MacGillivray's
   Warbler p. 161
American
   Redstart p. 160
Canada Warbler p. 165
Hooded Warbler p. 164

Common
   Yellowthroat p. 166
Magnolia Warbler p. 168
Yellow-rumped
   Warbler p. 169
Palm Warbler p. 168
Yellow Warbler p. 170
Black-throated Green
   Warbler p. 170
Yellow-throated
   Warbler p. 172
Blackburnian
   Warbler p. 173
Pine Warbler p. 174
American
   Goldfinch p. 193

MEDIUM
Northern Flicker p. 107
Western Kingbird p 111
Great Crested
   Flycatcher p. 112
Horned Lark p. 120
Yellow-breasted
   Chat p. 167
Western
   Meadowlark p. 177
Yellow-headed
   Blackbird p. 179
Scott's Oriole p. 183
Evening Grosbeak p. 187

Blue

*prominent
color or markings*

SMALL
Eastern Bluebird p. 151
Mountain Bluebird p.150
Northern Parula p.159

Black-throated Blue
   Warbler p.172
Blue Grosbeak p.186
Indigo Bunting p.188

MEDIUM
Blue Jay p.122
Scrub Jay p.123

LARGE
Belted Kingfisher p.92
Steller's Jay p. 122

Long Tail

SMALL
Barn Swallow *p. 127*
Wrentit *p. 131*
Blue gray
    Gnatcatcher *p. 155*

MEDIUM
American Kestrel *p. 84*
Mockingbird *p. 142*
Gray Catbird *p. 143*

Brown Thrasher *p. 144*
California Thrasher *p. 145*
Sage Thrasher *p. 144*

LARGE
*Northern Pintail *p. 39*
*Forster's Tern *p. 72*
*Common Tern *p. 72*
Sharp-shinned Hawk *p. 78*
Marsh Hawk *p. 84*
Prairie Falcon *p. 85*
Peregrine Falcon *p. 85*

Sharp-tailed Grouse *p. 87*
Mourning Dove *p. 91*
Yellow-billed
    Cuckoo *p. 92*
Greater Roadrunner *p. 93*
Scissor-tailed
    Flycatcher *p. 113*
Black-billed Magpie *p. 124*
Common Grackle *p. 180*

VERY LARGE
Ring-necked
    Pheasant *p. 88*

Very Long Bill

SMALL
Ruby throated
    Hummingbird *p. 102*
Anna's
    Hummingbird *p. 102*
Rufous
    Hummingbird *p. 103*
Black-chinned
    Hummingbird *p. 103*

MEDIUM
*Virginia Rail *p. 32*
*Long-billed
    Dowitcher *p. 56*
*Dunlin *p. 57*
*Common Snipe *p. 60*
American
    Woodcock *p. 60*
California Thrasher *p. 145*

LARGE
*Northern Shoveler *p. 40*
*American
    Oystercatcher *p. 46*

*American Avocet *p. 46*
*Black-necked Stilt *p. 47*
Long-billed Curlew *p. 48*
*Marbled Godwit *p. 49*
*Black Skimmer *p. 73*

VERY LARGE
*Brown Pelican *p. 18*
*American White
    Pelican *p. 19*
*Great Blue Heron *p. 22*
*Great Egret *p. 25*
*Wood Stork *p. 29*
*Glossy Ibis *p. 26*
*Roseate Spoonbill *p. 28*

Crest or Tufts

SMALL
Tufted Titmouse *p. 130*

MEDIUM
California Quail *p. 88*
Scaled Quail *p. 88*
Eastern Screech-owl *p. 99*
Horned Lark *p. 120*

Blue Jay *p. 122*
Cedar Waxwing *p. 153*
Phainopepla *p. 152*
Northern Cardinal *p. 186*

LARGE
*Horned Grebe *p.17*
*Wood Duck *p. 40*
*Hooded Merganser *p. 45*
*Tufted Puffin *p. 77*
Ruffed Grouse *p. 86*

Greater Roadrunner *p. 93*
Belted Kingfisher *p. 92*
Great Horned Owl *p. 96*
Long-eared Owl *p. 98*
Pileated
    Woodpecker *p. 105*
Steller's Jay *p. 122*

VERY LARGE
*Common
    Merganser *p. 45*

Birds That Cling to Tree Trunks

SMALL
Downy
   Woodpecker p. 109
White-breasted
   Nuthatch p. 132
Red-breasted
   Nuthatch p. 132

Brown Creeper p. 132
Black-and-White
   Warbler p. 158

MEDIUM
Red-bellied
   Woodpecker p. 106
Red-headed
   Woodpecker p. 106
Acorn
   Woodpecker p. 104

Northern Flicker p. 107
Yellow-bellied
   Sapsucker p. 108
Hairy
   Woodpecker p. 109
Three-toed
   Woodpecker p. 108

LARGE
Pileated
   Woodpecker p. 105

Hovering Birds

SMALL
Ruby throated
   Hummingbird p. 102
Anna's
   Hummingbird p. 102

Rufous
   Hummingbird p. 103
Black-chinned
   Hummingbird p. 103

MEDIUM
*Least Tern p. 74
*Black Tern p. 74

American Kestrel p. 84
*Belted Kingfisher p. 92

LARGE
*Forster's Tern p. 72
Common Tern p. 72
Red-tailed Hawk p. 79
*Osprey p. 82

Soaring and Gliding Birds

SMALL
Chimney Swift p. 100
White-throated
   Swift p. 101
Tree Swallow p. 126
Barn Swallow p. 127

MEDIUM
Purple Martin p. 128

LARGE
*Ring-billed Gull p. 67
*Herring Gull p. 67

Red-tailed Hawk p. 79
Red-shouldered
   Hawk p. 80
Swainson's Hawk p. 81
*Osprey p. 82
Marsh Hawk p. 84
Short-eared Owl p. 98

VERY LARGE
*Brown Pelican p. 18
*American White
   Pelican p. 19
*Great Blue
   Heron p. 22
*Great Egret p. 25
*Wood Stork p. 29
Sandhill Crane p. 31
*Great Black-backed
   Gull p. 68
Turkey Vulture p. 78
Golden Eagle p. 82
*Bald Eagle p. 83

*associated mainly with water

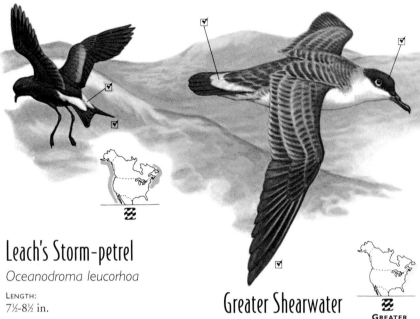

Leach's Storm-petrel

Oceanodroma leucorhoa

LENGTH:
7½-8½ in.

WHAT TO LOOK FOR:
small dark seabird; tail forked; rump white (dark in southern California); butterflylike flight.

HABITAT:
open seas; islands (breeding).

Storm-petrels are among the smallest and most aquatic oceanic birds. They spend most of the year on the open sea, pattering over the waves with their webbed feet, and approach land only to breed. Leach's Storm-petrels, like the closely related Wilson's Storm-petrels (*Oceanites oceanicus*), nest in colonies. Each female lays a single egg at the end of a tunnel. Parents alternate turns at incubation; one parent stays underground while the other seeks tiny fish and crustaceans at sea.

Greater Shearwater

GREATER SHEARWATER

Puffinus gravis

LENGTH:
17½-19½ in.

WHAT TO LOOK FOR:
long, narrow wings; dark cap; white on tail; alternately flaps and glides.

HABITAT: open seas.

SOOTY SHEARWATER

The name shearwater reflects the way these seabirds skim along the waves in search of fish and squid swimming just beneath the surface. They also chase prey underwater, using their long wings to propel themselves. In spring, after nesting more than 2,500 miles south of the equator, thousands of Greater Shearwaters migrate into the northern Atlantic. A second species, the Sooty Shearwater (*Puffinus griseus*), migrates over both the Atlantic and the Pacific.

BREEDING

Common Loon

Gavia immer

LENGTH:
28-30 in.

WHAT TO LOOK FOR:
large, heavy body; pointed bill; dark
head, prominent neck ring, and black
and white pattern on back (breeding);
upper parts dark gray in winter.

HABITAT:
forest-edged lakes, rivers, coasts.

The far-carrying laughs and yodels of the Common Loon are among the most extraordinary sounds in nature. Although this bird is a strong flier, it can take off only from
water—and a large body of water at that. Its legs are set so far back that it walks poorly,
but once afloat the loon is completely at home. It occasionally rides with bill and eyes
dipped below the surface, as if scouting, then dives in the wink of an eye. A loon can
swim long distances underwater, now and again poking its bill above the surface for air.
Like the Common Loon, the smaller Red-throated Loon (*Gavia stellata*) winters mainly
along the coast.

Western Grebe

Aechmophorus occidentalis

LENGTH:
20-25 in.

WHAT TO LOOK FOR:
large size; neck long, slender; black cap; bill pointed, greenish.

HABITAT:
lakes with reedy edges; coasts (mainly in winter).

These elegant "swan grebes" of western lakes and sloughs build floating nests anchored to reeds. Before nesting, Western Grebes perform a variety of courtship dances on the water. Swimming side by side, male and female rhythmically arch their necks, the head of each bird repeatedly touching its back. Also side by side, they race across the surface with heads thrust forward and bodies held upright. Clark's Grebe (*Aechmophorus clarkii*), which occupies the same range as the Western, differs in having the white on the cheek extending above the eye, and in having a yellow bill.

Horned Grebe

Podiceps auritus

LENGTH:
12-15 in.

WHAT TO LOOK FOR:
small size; short neck; thin bill; golden "horns" (breeding); white cheek and neck (nonbreeding).

HABITAT:
lakes, ponds, marshes; coasts (winter).

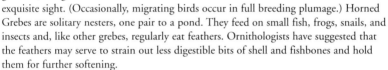

NONBREEDING

BREEDING

On the waters of its northern breeding grounds, this golden-horned bird is an exquisite sight. (Occasionally, migrating birds occur in full breeding plumage.) Horned Grebes are solitary nesters, one pair to a pond. They feed on small fish, frogs, snails, and insects and, like other grebes, regularly eat feathers. Ornithologists have suggested that the feathers may serve to strain out less digestible bits of shell and fishbones and hold them for further softening.

Pied-billed Grebe

Podilymbus podiceps

LENGTH:
12-15 in.

WHAT TO LOOK FOR:
small size; thick neck; white undertail; bill short, with black ring near tip (breeding).

HABITAT:
ponds, marshes with open water; bays, coves (winter).

Water Witch and Hell-diver are old-time names for this chunky bird, which can sink underwater with startling swiftness by forcing air out of its body and compressing the feathers. Like the young of other grebes, the soft, striped Pied-billed Grebe chicks are excellent divers from the time of hatching. Chicks riding piggyback on a parent may stay aboard even when the adult dives, perhaps holding on to the parent's feathers with their bills.

IMMATURE

Brown Pelican

Pelecanus occidentalis

SIZE:
length, 3½-4½ ft.; wingspan, 7 ft.

WHAT TO LOOK FOR:
large, bulky bird with large, bulky bill; gray-brown body; whitish head; red-brown neck with white stripe (breeding); flies with alternate flaps and glides.

HABITAT:
usually in ocean or brackish water.

The Brown Pelican sights its prey while in flight, then dives with bill closed and enters the water in a burst of spray. At that moment it lifts its upper mandible and opens its pouch outward, forming a scoop. Once the fish is safe inside—along with water twice the weight of the bird—the bill shuts, and the pelican bobs to the surface. The bird may take less than 2 seconds to make its catch. A minute or so may pass while it floats with bill pointed downward, evidently waiting for water to drain out so it can swallow the fish. Louisiana is sometimes called the Pelican State, although the pelican population in that state has been drastically depleted.

American White Pelican

Pelecanus erythrorhynchos

SIZE:
length, 4-5 ft.; wingspan, 9 ft.

WHAT TO LOOK FOR:
plumage white except for black on wings; bill and pouch pinkish-orange (gray on immature).

HABITAT:
lakes, ponds; when not breeding, in coastal bays.

Many observers remark on the seemingly military behavior of pelican flocks. Flying American White Pelicans usually flap their wings and glide in unison. Over long distances they proceed in straight lines or in V's. A group may sun on a sandspit, all facing in the same direction, all bills pointed to the sky. "Should one chance to gape," wrote Audubon, "all, as if by sympathy, in succession open their... mandibles, yawning lazily and ludicrously." When fishing, American White Pelicans form a line in the water and swim toward the beach, beating the water with their wings and herding the fish ahead of them. Unlike Brown Pelicans, they do not dive.

Double-crested Cormorant

Phalacrocorax auritus

LENGTH: 2½-3 ft.

WHAT TO LOOK FOR:
large dark bird; thin bill; orange on throat; whitish breast and buffy belly on immature; often stands with wings outspread.

HABITAT: coasts; freshwater.

Flocks of migrating Double-crested Cormorants can be mistaken for Canada Geese. But instead of flapping steadily and honking as they fly, cormorants flap for a while and then sail. They are silent in flight. Like loons and grebes, they fish by diving from the surface. Cormorants breed in colonies, chiefly on rocky islands and in groves of trees and bushes. Their nests, constructed of sticks and other plant materials, may be garnished with feathers and sprigs of greenery.

Northern Gannet

Morus bassanus

SIZE:
length, 3-3½ ft.; wingspan, 6 ft.

WHAT TO LOOK FOR:
wings long, pointed, black-tipped; tail pointed; white body (gray-brown on immature); head pale orange; bill long, conical.

HABITAT:
oceans, offshore islands.

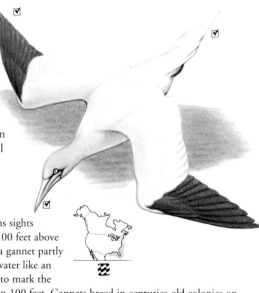

This cousin of cormorants and pelicans sights schools of fish from heights of 80 to 100 feet above the surface. When diving on its prey, a gannet partly closes its wings and plunges into the water like an artillery shell, leaving a geyser behind to mark the spot. It can reportedly dive deeper than 100 feet. Gannets breed in centuries-old colonies on both sides of the Atlantic. The largest one in North America is on Bonaventure Island, off the Gaspé Peninsula in Quebec.

MALE

FEMALE

Anhinga

Anhinga anhinga

LENGTH:
about 3 ft.

WHAT TO LOOK FOR:
neck long, sinuous; pointed bill; wings streaked with
white; female browner, with whitish throat.

HABITAT:
slow-moving fresh or brackish water; occasionally in
protected saltwater areas.

The Snakebird, or Water Turkey, frequently assumes a spread-wing pose when ashore, as
do certain other species. The posture may help some birds to regulate body temperature
or to balance themselves. Anhingas are believed to hold out their wings to dry—a neces-
sity because of the porous nature of their feathers, which absorb more water than the
oilier plumage of ducks and grebes. An Anhinga spends much time swimming with just
its snakelike head and neck above water. It eats everything from frogs' eggs and insects to
fish and small alligators.

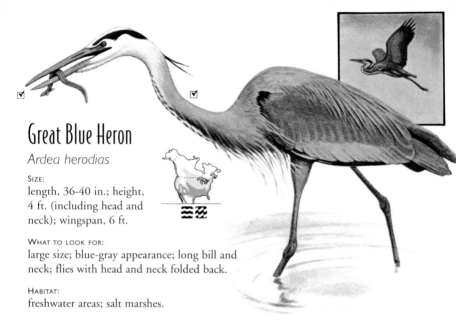

Great Blue Heron

Ardea herodias

SIZE:
length, 36-40 in.; height,
4 ft. (including head and
neck); wingspan, 6 ft.

WHAT TO LOOK FOR:
large size; blue-gray appearance; long bill and
neck; flies with head and neck folded back.

HABITAT:
freshwater areas; salt marshes.

This wary and powerful bird spears fish or catches them by using its bill like scissors. It also
feeds on frogs, snakes, mice, and birds. A Great Blue Heron may slowly stalk its prey or stand
motionless waiting for something to come within reach. Though bulky, it can float like a
goose and take off from the surface of the water. It nests in colonies, usually in tall trees.
Ornithologists have recently concluded that the "Great White Heron," found in Florida,
the West Indies, and Mexico, is actually an all-white version of the Great Blue Heron and
not a separate species.

Green Heron

Butorides virescens

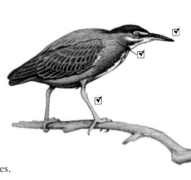

LENGTH:
18-22 in.

WHAT TO LOOK FOR:
small size; brownish appearance (white streaks on
underside of immature); red-brown neck; sharp-
pointed bill; orange legs.

HABITAT:
lakes, ponds, bogs, freshwater and saltwater marshes.

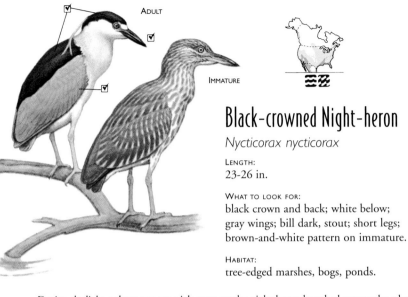

ADULT

IMMATURE

Black-crowned Night-heron

Nycticorax nycticorax

LENGTH:
23-26 in.

WHAT TO LOOK FOR:
black crown and back; white below;
gray wings; bill dark, stout; short legs;
brown-and-white pattern on immature.

HABITAT:
tree-edged marshes, bogs, ponds.

During daylight a sharp eye can pick out a stocky night-heron hunched over at the edge of a pond or in a nearby tree. Night-herons do most of their feeding between dusk and dawn. Although they are mainly fish eaters, a group of them nesting near a tern colony may prey on tern chicks and eggs after dark. A young Black-crowned Night-heron looks much like a young Yellow-crowned Night-heron (*Nycticorax violacea*), a less common species with an eastern range. But in flight part of the legs of the latter bird projects beyond the tail; the Black-crowned Night-heron shows only the feet.

◀ Green Heron (AT LEFT) This species is often seen poised motionless at the water's edge; it is a resourceful and even acrobatic fish catcher and also eats small land animals. It has been observed, for example, perched on a post and leaning down until most of its body was below its feet; from that position it snatched a fish, then righted itself to swallow. Occasionally the heron will dart from its perch and dive underwater after prey. And one individual was spotted apparently using a floating feather to attract small fish to the surface.

Snowy Egret

Great Egret

Snowy Egret

Egretta thula

LENGTH:
22-26 in.

WHAT TO LOOK FOR:
slim, white bird; filmy plumes
(breeding); black bill; legs black,
with bright yellow feet.

HABITAT:
tree-edged wetlands near shallow
fresh or brackish water.

Few birds rival the white egrets in the beauty of
their breeding plumage—a beauty that nearly
caused their extinction. (Both the Snowy Egret
and its larger relative, the Great Egret, were shot
by the thousands for their filmy plumes.) In spite
of the Snowy Egret's quick, darting motions and
golden "slippers," it is often confused with the
immature Little Blue Heron (*Egretta caerulea*), a
white bird with green legs and feet and a bluish
bill. The Reddish Egret (*Egretta rufescens*) has a
white phase as well.

Great Egret

Ardea alba

LENGTH:
36-42 in.

WHAT TO LOOK FOR:
large white bird; neck long,
thin, curved in flight; bill
orange-yellow; legs and feet
black.

HABITAT:
wetlands, wet pastures.

Egrets and herons nest in trees, frequently in
mixed colonies that include cormorants and ibises.
When the male Great Egret (also known as the
Common or American Egret) is ready to incubate
the eggs, he lands on a branch near the nest; as he
approaches, he raises his wings and the long nup-
tial plumes on his back. His mate reacts by raising
her back feathers as he caresses her with his head.
After the female leaves, the male settles on the
eggs, once more raising and flaring his plumes.

Glossy Ibis

Plegadis falcinellus

LENGTH: 19-26 in.

WHAT TO LOOK FOR:
overall dark appearance; bill long, curved downward; whitish neck and throat on immature.

HABITAT:
marshes, shallow ponds, salt or brackish lagoons.

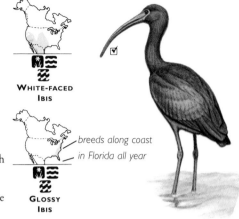

WHITE-FACED IBIS

breeds along coast in Florida all year

GLOSSY IBIS

This handsome bird with bronzy plumage has spread northward in recent years, as have the Cardinal and Northern Mockingbird. For most of this century colonies of Glossy Ibis were confined to Florida and the Gulf states, but now the species breeds along most of the Atlantic coast and strays into Canada. For feeding, the Glossy Ibis prefers a grassy marsh with shallow water. It probes in the mud with its long downward-curved bill, seeking crayfish and mollusks; it also takes insects, frogs, and small fish. A similar species, the less common White-faced Ibis (*Plegadis chihi*), is more western in range; the White Ibis (*Eudocimus albus*) is generally restricted to the Gulf Coast and southeastern states.

Cattle Egret

Bubulcus ibis

LENGTH:
18½-20 in.

WHAT TO LOOK FOR:
white bird; tawny areas; orange legs (breeding); orange or yellow bill.

HABITAT:
brushy areas, open fields.

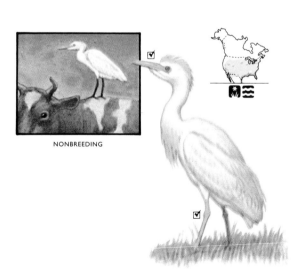

NONBREEDING

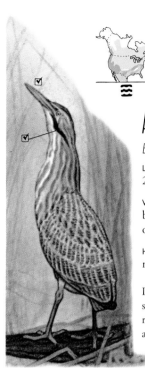

American Bittern

Botaurus lentiginosus

LENGTH:
25-30 in.

WHAT TO LOOK FOR:
brown and white pattern; white throat; black "whiskers"; outer wing areas dark in flight; yellowish bill.

HABITAT:
marshes, bogs, swamps; occasionally in salt marshes.

In the motionless "freeze" pose, with its bill pointing straight to the sky, the American Bittern blends into the reeds of its swampy habitat. Among the bird's nicknames are Thunder-pumper and Stake-driver. Both are references to its spring song, which sounds like an old-time water pump or, from a distance, a sledgehammer striking a stake. A bittern swallows air in several gulps, swelling its throat; then it violently constricts its thick neck muscles, expelling the air and producing the pumping sound.

◀ **Cattle Egret** (AT LEFT) Until late in the 19th century this species was found only in the Old World. Then it began a remarkable range expansion that is still under way. Just how Cattle Egrets crossed the Atlantic (whether by boat or on the wing) is still a question. In any case, they first appeared in South America about 1880, nested in Florida in 1952, and spread rapidly into other states. Often they associate with grazing animals, feeding on insects stirred up by the hooves. They also follow farm tractors, which perform a similar service for these opportunistic birds.

in Florida,
western Gulf,
and western
Mexico

Roseate Spoonbill

Ajaia ajaja

LENGTH:
30-33 in.

WHAT TO LOOK FOR:
spoon-shaped bill; general
pink and white coloration;
immature white with
yellowish legs.

HABITAT:
mangrove swamps, coastal
islands, shallow lagoons.

A spoonbill moves its partly opened bill from side to side through water or mud, feeling for its prey. When it encounters small fish, shrimp, or shellfish, it snaps its bill shut. If the catch is a fish, the bird may beat it on the water before swallowing. Roseate Spoonbills build stick nests in trees, frequently in company with herons, egrets, cormorants, ibises, and Anhingas. Mainly residents of Florida, the Gulf Coast, and areas to the south, the spoonbills were once much more common than they are today. In the past they were shot for their wings, which were made into fans; today their habitat continues to be reduced. Everglades National Park in Florida and areas near Rockport, Texas, are prime places to see the birds.

Wood Stork

Mycteria americana

SIZE:
length, 36-42 in.; wingspan, 5½ ft.

WHAT TO LOOK FOR:
large white bird; head and neck blackish, bare-skinned;
bill long, heavy, tapering; black flight feathers.

HABITAT:
swamps, marshy meadows, shallow freshwater areas.

This species, formerly called the Wood Ibis, is the only stork in North America. Among the stork's nicknames are Gourdhead and Flinthead, references to the bare, dark skin covering the head and upper neck. Young storks, unlike their parents, are feathered in those areas. Another difference is in voice; although older storks are mostly silent, the young birds produce an unbelievable clamor. One observer heard the grunts, squeals, bleats, and bellows coming from a Wood Stork colony and thought at first that the tremendous uproar was made by Bullfrogs and alligators, for "it hardly seemed credible that birds should make such a noise."

Whooping Crane
Grus americana

SIZE:
length, 4-4½ ft.; wingspan, 7-7½ ft.

WHAT TO LOOK FOR:
large white bird (immature tawny);
black on wings; red often visible on head.

HABITAT:
northern bogs, grasslands, marshes.

This magnificent bird takes its name from its penetrating, bugling voice. The Whooping Crane is a wary bird, with long legs and neck that permit it to see long distances across the marshes. Despite its wariness, it was always an irresistible target for hunters, and fewer than two dozen Whooping Cranes remained in the wild by the 1940s. Although the breeding range once included much of central North America, the species now nests only in a remote area (Wood Buffalo National Park) in northwestern Canada. Whooping Cranes are slowly increasing in number, thanks to intensive conservation efforts. Since 1993, about 100 juveniles have been released in central Florida in an attempt to establish a non-migratory flock. Wintering Whooping Cranes in small family groups can be readily seen at the Aransas National Wildlife Refuge in Texas.

Sandhill Crane

Grus canadensis

SIZE:
length, 3-4 ft.; wingspan, 6½-7 ft.

WHAT TO LOOK FOR:
tall gray bird
(immature pinkish brown);
reddish cap.

HABITAT:
tundra, marshes, grasslands; grainfields (migration, winter).

All of the cranes are spectacular dancers. The Sandhill Crane bows, droops its wings, skips, hops, and leaps as high as 15 or 20 feet into the air. Pairs perform together during courtship, but dancing is confined neither to the breeding season nor to pairs; hundreds of birds may dance at the same time. Cranes nest on mounds of vegetation, often surrounded by water. The female usually lays two eggs, and young birds stay with their parents for nearly a year. Cranes eat amphibians, reptiles, insects, and small mammals, as well as fruits, grain, and other plant material.

Virginia Rail

Rallus limicola

LENGTH:
9-11 in.

WHAT TO LOOK FOR:
long bill; orange legs; brownish-red breast; flanks barred with white; undertail white.

HABITAT:
freshwater marshes; salt marshes (mainly in winter).

North America's rails are elusive birds that generally manage to escape notice. Except in migration, they seldom fly if they can walk. The Virginia Rail usually stays airborne for only a few yards, then drops into the marsh grass and runs into hiding. The King Rail (*Rallus elegans*) of freshwater marshes and the Clapper Rail (*Rallus longirostris*) of salt marshes resemble this species in coloring but are about twice as large.

Sora

Porzana carolina

LENGTH:
9-10 in.

WHAT TO LOOK FOR:
small trim bird; short bill; black face and throat; flanks barred with white; undertail white; legs yellow-green.

HABITAT:
wet grassland, swamps; salt marshes (mainly in winter).

Though it is seldom seen, the Sora is actually our commonest rail. Like others of its family, it prefers walking to flying; its compressed body enables it to slip between reed stalks without betraying its passage. It feeds on small mollusks, insects, and seeds, notably wild rice. Vocalizations include a rising whistle and a musical descending call.

Common Moorhen

Gallinula chloropus

LENGTH:
12-14 in.

WHAT TO LOOK FOR:
dark ducklike bird; frontal shield red (whitish on immature); bill red, yellow-tipped; white along flanks and undertail.

HABITAT:
weedy edges of rivers, lakes, ponds, marshes.

The moorhens, along with the rails and coots, belong to the Rallidae, a worldwide family of some 130 species. The Common Moorhen, formerly called the Common Gallinule, has a larger range and is more abundant than the colorful Purple Gallinule (*Porphyrula martinica*) of the southeastern states. Both species swim well, with a characteristic pumping motion of the head. They also move about by walking on floating lily pads.

American Coot

Fulica americana

LENGTH:
13-15 in.

WHAT TO LOOK FOR:
dark ducklike bird; white bill and frontal shield; whitish undertail.

HABITAT:
lakes, ponds, marshes, grasslands near water; bays, estuaries (winter).

Unlike certain kinds of ducks, coots cannot spring into the air from the water's surface. Instead, they patter along on top of the water into the wind until they achieve sufficient lift. Usually, however, they do not bother to take flight; they simply dash to safety farther from shore or disappear into the nearest stand of reeds.

Mute Swan

Cygnus olor

LENGTH:
4½-5 ft.

WHAT TO LOOK FOR:
large white bird (immature gray); neck held in S-curve; bill orange, with black tip; black knob at base of upper mandible.

 *all year*

HABITAT:
lakes, pond, marshes, sheltered coastal areas.

Many years ago Mute Swans were brought to North America from Europe. Some escaped from captivity in the New York area and gave rise to a wild population, which has slowly expanded its range. Mute Swans feed on aquatic plants and insects. The nest, built near water or among reeds in the shallows, is a mound of vegetation 3 or 4 feet across. Up to a dozen young (called cygnets) hatch in the depression on top. Mute Swans are not really mute: the cygnets peep, and the adults sometimes hiss or grunt. In flight the stroking of the great wings produces a far-carrying hum.

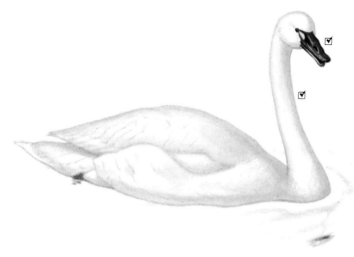

Tundra Swan

Cygnus columbianus

LENGTH:
4-4½ ft.

WHAT TO LOOK FOR:
large white bird (immature gray); neck held
straight; bill black, usually with yellow spot.

HABITAT:
tundra lakes, grassland pools; estuaries (winter).

This stately bird, formerly known as the Whistling Swan, is the most widespread swan
in North America. It nests in the Far North, but thousands winter on both the Atlantic
and Pacific coasts, as well as on lakes in the interior. During spring and fall its call—not
a whistle but a mellow, musical honking—is heard from large flocks as they travel to or
from the breeding grounds on the tundra.

BLUE PHASE

WHITE PHASE

Snow Goose

Chen caerulescens

LENGTH:
24-30 in.

WHAT TO LOOK FOR:
white bird with black wing tips
(white phase); dark body with
white head and neck (blue phase).

HABITAT:
tundra ponds, lakes; grasslands,
saltwater (migration).

From the time they hatch, the two types of Snow Goose are distinct. White-phase goslings are yellowish; blue-phase, olive-green. Audubon believed the blue-phase birds to be immatures; later they were considered a separate species. It was not until 1929 that a nesting area of "Blue Geese" was discovered north of Hudson Bay. By observing nesting birds, scientists learned that the two phases interbreed, and that there is an intermediate phase. They are now considered members of the same species.

Canada Goose

Branta canadensis

LENGTH:
22-40 in.

WHAT TO LOOK FOR:
white area on cheek; dark neck, back, and tail; white undertail.

HABITAT:
ponds, lakes, bays, estuaries, grasslands.

North America's commonest goose ranges in size from the small "cackling" race, weighing as little as 2 pounds, to the "giant" race, of up to 18 pounds. Canada Geese nest in all sorts of places. The usual sites are near the water's edge on a moderately elevated platform, such as a small island or muskrat house, but some birds nest on rock ledges in cliffs or in the abandoned tree nests of other large birds. Man's successful efforts at conserving this species have radically changed its migration habits. Wildlife refuges in the central states, for example, now hold many thousands of wintering geese that would previously have traveled much farther south.

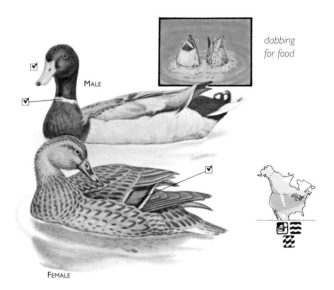

dabbing
for food

MALE

FEMALE

Mallard

Anas platyrhynchos

LENGTH:
16-24 in.

WHAT TO LOOK FOR:
head and neck of male glossy green, with white ring; female brown overall; blue speculum (band on wing); yellow or orange bill.

HABITAT:
shallow ponds, marshes; sheltered saltwater (winter).

The commonest duck in the world breeds in Europe, Asia, and North America. Remarkably adaptable to civilization, it will breed in a city park if there is even a small pond. Mallards usually nest near the water's edge, but occasionally they choose a site on higher ground. When the ducks are agitated, they can leap upward from the water into flight and then almost hover in midair before selecting an escape route. Mallards are often seen with just the ends of their tails sticking up out of shallow water as they feed on the plants and small animals found at the bottom. They also eat grain and other foods.

Black Duck

Anas rubripes

LENGTH: 20-23 in.

WHAT TO LOOK FOR:
dark body; silvery wing linings; bluish-purple speculum; yellow to green bill.

HABITAT:
shallow ponds, lakes, marshes; sheltered saltwater (winter).

A Black Duck usually lays 10 to 12 eggs. When a chick is ready to break out of the shell, it chips a row of holes around one end. Eventually the "cap" gives way, and the duckling pushes out—first its head, then one wing, then the other. Finally it lies completely out of the shell, exhausted and naked except for a few scattered dark hairs. As the chick dries, these hairs split open; out of each pops a down feather as big as a fingertip. Within a short time a fluffy duckling is ready to follow its mother out of the nest.

Northern Pintail

Anas acuta

LENGTH: 20-30 in.

WHAT TO LOOK FOR:
neck long; male with white stripe on neck and long pointed tail; female mottled brown with shorter tail.

HABITAT:
lakes, ponds, marshes; sheltered saltwater (winter).

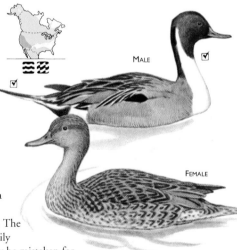

MALE

FEMALE

This slender, graceful duck has as broad a nesting range as the Mallard. Like the Mallard, it is a tip-up, or dabbling, duck. The stripe on the male's neck makes him readily identifiable at a distance, but females may be mistaken for other kinds of ducks. Between the breeding season and fall migration, the males (drakes) of many species molt their feathers and develop an "eclipse" plumage, in which they look much like the females. The Pintail drake becomes a browner and darker version of his mate.

Northern Shoveler

Anas clypeata

LENGTH: 17-22 in.

WHAT TO LOOK FOR:
bill long, shovel-shaped; blue wing patch
(not always obvious); male with green head and brown side patch;
female mottled brown.

HABITAT: muddy creeks, marshes; shallow saltwater (winter).

MALE

Twice as wide at the tip as at the base, the specialized bill of the shoveler sets it apart from other ducks. As the name implies, the bird uses the bill like a shovel to collect the mud and water from which it strains out its food. Its diet includes snails, water insects, and such small aquatic plants as duckweed. The shoveler usually nests close to water. In a plant-lined depression the female lays from 8 to 12 eggs at the rate of an egg a day. As the laying goes on, she plucks down from her body and adds it to the nest. She does not start incubating until the last egg is laid.

Wood Duck

Aix sponsa

LENGTH: 18-21 in.

WHAT TO LOOK FOR: white throat and facial pattern ("spectacles" on female); crest (not always obvious).

HABITAT: forest-edged lakes, ponds, swamps, marshes.

Unless you are on the lookout for this colorful bird, you may hear rather than see it as it flies off quickly through the woods, crying *weep, weep, weep.* Wood Duck females nest in tree cavities or in man-made nest boxes. Up to 15 eggs are laid on a bed of white down and incubated by the female for about four weeks. Soon after hatching, the ducklings jump from the nest hole in response to the call of their mother. If the nesting tree is in an upland area, she then leads her brood to water. Wood Ducks are not the only tree-nesting ducks; Buffleheads, Hooded Mergansers, Goldeneyes, and several kinds of whistling (tree) ducks also nest in tree cavities.

FEMALE

MALE

Green-winged Teal
Anas crecca

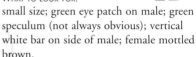

LENGTH:
12-16 in.

WHAT TO LOOK FOR:
small size; green eye patch on male; green speculum (not always obvious); vertical white bar on side of male; female mottled brown.

HABITAT:
shallow ponds, lakes, streams, marshes; sheltered saltwater (occasionally in winter).

BLUE-WINGED TEAL (MALE)

GREEN-WINGED TEAL (MALE)

Compact, speeding flocks of little Green-winged Teal turn and twist as if they were controlled by a single force. These birds winter mostly in the southern states and in Mexico, although some remain as far north as Alaska and the Great Lakes. A close relative, the Blue-winged Teal (*Anas discors*), usually winters south of the border; some individuals may cover 7,000 miles as they migrate between northern Canada and southern South America. Blue-winged Teal are generally among the last ducks to arrive on the nesting grounds and the first to leave.

American Wigeon
Anas americana

LENGTH:
18-24 in.

WHAT TO LOOK FOR:
head of male white on top, with green patch; large white wing patch; white underparts; black tail on male; female brownish above, pale tawny on sides.

HABITAT:
ponds, lakes, rivers, irrigated land; sheltered saltwater (winter).

MALE

Often called Baldpate because of its snowy cap, the American Wigeon feeds in shallow water, tipping up like the Mallard, Pintail, and other dabbling ducks. Wigeons are sometimes found in the company of coots, scaup, and other diving birds, feeding on the deeper-growing plants that these divers have brought to the surface. As they forage, wigeon may also eat small animals (insects and snails) and young grass. The sounds they make differ according to sex. The male whistles, usually in a quick three-note series—*whew, whew, whew*; the female growls and quacks.

REDHEAD

Canvasback
Aythya valisineria

LENGTH:
19-24 in.

WHAT TO LOOK FOR:
head with "ski-slope" profile; male with red-brown head and pale back; female with brown head, neck, and breast.

HABITAT:
lakes, ponds, marshes; sheltered saltwater (winter).

MALE

Even at a distance, this handsome duck can be recognized by its long neck and the distinctive profile of its head and bill. The Canvasback is a deep diver, reaching depths of up to 30 feet in its search for small invertebrates and the roots of aquatic plants. Canvasbacks are often found together with Redheads (*Aythya americana*). Though superficially similar, the Redhead has a shorter neck, rounder head, and grayer back.

Ring-necked Duck
Aythya collaris

LENGTH:
15-18 in.

WHAT TO LOOK FOR:
bill bluish, with white ring, black tip, and white at base; male with purple gloss on head, black back, and white bar on side; female brown, with white eye-ring and streak to nape.

HABITAT:
forest-edged lakes, ponds, rivers, marshes; sheltered saltwater (winter).

FEMALE

MALE

On a gray spring morning, when the ice has just melted in a northern pond, a male Ring-necked Duck riding on the dark waters blends into the subtle tints of its setting. The ring on the bird's neck is virtually invisible, and the species might better have been named for the prominent ring around the bill. In flight the Ring-necked Duck can be distinguished from the scaups by its inconspicuous wing stripe.

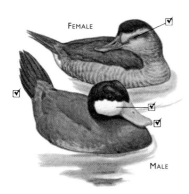

FEMALE

MALE

Ruddy Duck

Oxyura jamaicensis

LENGTH:
14-17 in.

WHAT TO LOOK FOR:
dark cap; large white cheek patch (female with dark slash); blue bill (breeding male); tail short, spiky, usually erect.

HABITAT:
lakes, ponds, rivers, marshes; saltwater (winter).

In the breeding season the richly colored male puts on a remarkable display. He erects the stiff feathers of his tail until they nearly touch the back of his head, flares the feathers over his eyes into "horns," puffs up his neck and breast, and drums on his throat with his bright blue bill. The drumming forces air from his breast feathers so that the water bubbles in front of him. The female usually makes her nest among such standing plants as rushes, which she pulls over to make a sort of roof. The eggs are huge for such a small duck—bigger than those of the Canvasback, which is much larger than a Ruddy Duck.

Lesser Scaup

Aythya affinis

LENGTH: 14-18 in.

WHAT TO LOOK FOR: blue bill; white wing stripe; male with purple gloss on head; female with white at bill.

HABITAT: ponds, lakes, marshes; sheltered saltwater (winter).

The Little Bluebill, as old-time hunters called this small diving duck, breeds near small prairie lakes and ponds. Lesser Scaup winter in freshwater or occasionally in protected coastal seas, typically forming dense masses known as rafts. Greater Scaup (*Aythya marila*) are strictly coastal in cold weather. The two scaups look quite similar, but the white wing stripe is more extensive on the Greater Scaup and the head has a green gloss.

FEMALE

MALE

FEMALE

FEMALE

MALE

MALE

Common Goldeneye
Bucephala clangula

LENGTH:
15½–20 in.

WHAT TO LOOK FOR:
male with glossy green head, round white patch below eye, black and white back and white belly; female mottled gray, with tawny head and white neck.

HABITAT:
rivers, lakes; open bays, estuaries (winter).

The nickname of this strikingly marked diving duck is Whistler, a reference to the ringing sound of its wings in flight. The courtship display of the Common Goldeneye is spectacular. While the male is snapping his head violently back and forth, his mate may lie on the water as if dead. Barrow's Goldeneye (*Bucephala islandica*), common in the West but rare elsewhere, is similar in appearance but is blacker and has a white crescent in front of the eye, and a purplish head. Both goldeneyes nest in cavities in trees.

Bufflehead
Bucephala albeola

LENGTH:
12–16 in.

WHAT TO LOOK FOR:
small size; white head patch; in flight, bold pattern on male and white wing patch on female.

HABITAT:
ponds, lakes, rivers; sheltered saltwater (winter).

The Bufflehead is as lively in courtship as the goldeneye. The male puffs out his snowy crown for extra visibility, snaps his head back and forth, and stands erect with beating wings. When nesting, the female usually chooses a tree cavity excavated by a flicker or other woodpecker. The opening may be only 3 inches in diameter, but somehow the chunky little duck (also known as the Butterball) manages to squeeze in and lay her eggs. The name Bufflehead comes from the little duck's big-headed appearance, which reminded early observers of the buffalo.

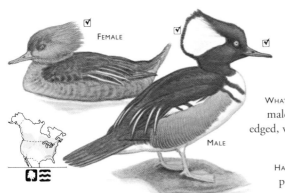

Hooded Merganser

Lophodytes cucullatus

LENGTH: 16-20 in.

WHAT TO LOOK FOR: narrow, dark bill; male with white breast and black-edged, white crest; female with tawny crest and gray breast.

HABITAT: forest-edged lakes, rivers, ponds, marshes; occasionally in saltwater.

Both male and female Hooded Mergansers have rounded, fan-shaped crests. When swimming they hold their crests partly closed (the male fully expands his showy topknot in courtship display). Hooded Mergansers in flight look very different, for their crests are laid completely back. These handsome ducks nest in tree cavities in swampy, woody country, often returning to the nest site of the previous year. They are good divers and feed on the bottom as well as at the surface.

Common Merganser

Mergus merganser

LENGTH:
21-27 in.

WHAT TO LOOK FOR:
long, slim body; thin reddish bill; male with dark green head and white breast; female with reddish head and shaggy crest.

HABITAT:
lakes, ponds, marshes, rivers in forested areas; open freshwater, sheltered saltwater (winter).

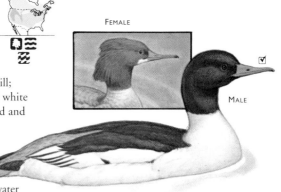

This fish duck often behaves like a loon or grebe. Hunting for food, it dips its bill and eyes below the surface; it dives well and can ride high or low in the water. Its nickname is Sawbill, a reference to the serrations that help it catch and hold fish. Partial to freshwater, the Common Merganser will remain there in winter if fish are plentiful and waters stay open.

American Oystercatcher

Haematopus palliatus

LENGTH:
17-20 in.

WHAT TO LOOK FOR:
large size; pied pattern;
long red bill; white wing
stripe prominent in flight.

AMERICAN
OYSTERCATCHER

HABITAT:
coastal areas.

Oysters form only part of the diet of this strikingly
patterned bird. Both the American Oystercatcher and
its Pacific Coast relative, the Black Oystercatcher
(*Haematopus bachmani*), feed not only on bivalves
exposed at low tide but also on barnacles, limpets,
snails, and marine worms. The bills are used to break
and pry open shells, to probe in the sand, and to dislodge
small animals clinging to rocks. Oystercatchers nest in shallow
depressions, sometimes lining them with pebbles or bits of shell, plants, or driftwood.

American Avocet

Recurvirostra americana

LENGTH:
15-20 in.

WHAT TO LOOK FOR:
head and neck cinnamon (gray on
nonbreeding bird); bill long,
upturned; striking pattern in flight.

HABITAT:
marshes, mud flats, beaches, shallow
lakes, ponds.

Black-necked Stilt
Himantopus mexicanus

LENGTH:
13½–15½ in.

WHAT TO LOOK FOR:
tall, slim bird; long red legs; straight, thin bill; wings, back, and back of neck black; legs extended well behind when flying.

HABITAT:
shallow lakes, mud flats, marshes, rice fields, other irrigated areas.

Many shorebirds engage in distraction displays when their eggs or young are threatened. Black-necked Stilts are masters at confusing and drawing away an intruder. In one type of display the stilt crouches with its wings spread and quivering. Or it may bob up and down in shallow water, splashing with its body. It suddenly falls down as if it had broken a leg, then gets up, takes a few steps, and falls again. Since stilts nest in colonies, they often perform together, calling loudly in the process. Ornithologists believe that such displays probably originated in purposeless frenzies caused by the bird's inability to decide whether to run away or attack.

◀ **American Avocet** (AT LEFT) The avocet catches a variety of food with its long, upcurved bill. Sweeping the bill from side to side along the bottom, it finds some prey by touch. Aquatic insects are snatched from the surface; flying insects are caught in midair. Avocets nest in colonies, each female laying an average of four eggs in a slight hollow. If the sites are flooded, the birds may quickly build up the nests until they are a foot or more high. The chicks are long-legged like the adults, but their bills show only a faint upward turn at first. They are able to swim, dive, and feed themselves soon after hatching.

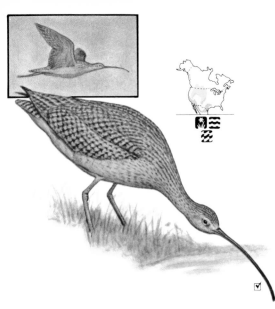

Long-billed Curlew
Numenius americanus

LENGTH:
20-24 in.

WHAT TO LOOK FOR:
large size; bill long, decurved; neck and legs moderately long; cinnamon wing linings visible in flight.

HABITAT:
dry prairies; farmlands, salt marshes, mud flats (migration, winter).

This is the largest North American shorebird, and its sickle-shaped bill is of a size to match. Originally the species nested on the central grasslands, and it suffered when prairies were turned into cropland. In areas that have been returned to grass for grazing purposes, the Long-billed Curlew is returning as well. Flocks of curlews fly high in migration, uttering the melodious whistle that suggests their name. In winter they are indeed shorebirds, for they feed on ocean beaches and salt meadows, where the slightly smaller Whimbrel (*Numenius phaeopus*) is also a common species.

Willet
Catoptrophorus
semipalmatus

LENGTH:
14-17 in.

WHAT TO LOOK FOR:
bill long, sturdy; mottled gray plumage; black and white wing pattern visible in flight.

HABITAT:
wetlands, moist prairies; salt marshes, beaches (winter).

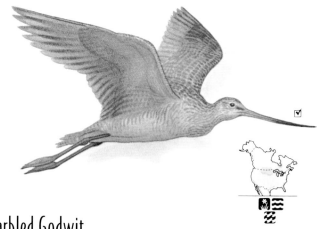

Marbled Godwit

Limosa fedoa

LENGTH:
16½-20 in.

WHAT TO LOOK FOR:
bill long, slightly upturned;
long legs; mottled above,
light cinnamon below;
red-brown patches on
underside of wing visible
in flight.

HABITAT:
prairies, wetlands; coastal
areas (winter).

The Marbled Godwit nests near water on
prairies, usually laying four eggs in a "saucer"
of dry grass. Its food is mainly aquatic—
snails, insects, small crustaceans. The species
was once much more widespread than it is
today. Gunning reduced its numbers, and the
conversion of prairies to cultivation drastically
restricted the territory available for nesting.
The smaller Hudsonian Godwit (*Limosa
haemastica*) has a white wing stripe and a
broad white band at the base of the tail. It
breeds in the Far North, migrates mainly
through the middle of the continent, and
winters in South America.

◀ **Willet** (AT LEFT) Birds often do the unexpected, thereby surprising observers who have
only a general familiarity with their habits. Although the Willet is a shorebird and so
might not be expected to perch on trees, bushes, and fences, often it does just that.
When landing it holds its dramatically marked wings above its head, as if poised for
flight. Willets are noisy birds. They often repeat their name —*pill-o-will-o-willet*—
but they also have a variety of sharper notes.

Greater Yellowlegs

Tringa melanoleuca

LENGTH:
12-15 in.

WHAT TO LOOK FOR:
long yellow legs; bill slender, rather
long; mottled gray back; white rump
and barred tail visible in flight.

HABITAT:
bogs, marshes, streams, ponds, tidal
flats (migration, winter).

With its loud, whistled call (a series of three to five notes), the Greater Yellowlegs is
one of the noisiest of the sandpipers. Old-timers called it Tattler or Tell-tale, for its
cries signaled the approach of an intruder. During migration this long-legged bird
may be seen dashing after minnows in a shallow pool or feeding with other shorebirds
on a mud flat. Smaller and with a proportionately shorter, thinner bill, the Lesser
Yellowlegs (*Tringa flavipes*) is best identified by the one- or two-syllable call.

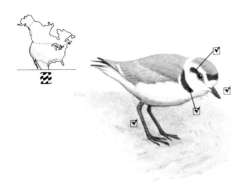

Snowy Plover

Charadrius alexandrinus

LENGTH:
6-7 in.

WHAT TO LOOK FOR:
pale color; dark streak at side of
neck; black spot behind eye; dark
legs and bill.

HABITAT:
beaches, salt flats, other open areas
near water.

Semipalmated Plover

Charadrius semipalmatus

LENGTH:
6-8 in.

WHAT TO LOOK FOR:
stocky, short-necked bird; black bar across chest; short bill; orange legs.

HABITAT:
tundra; lakeshores, mud flats, beaches.

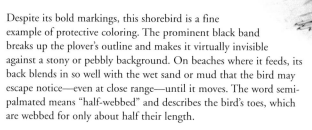

Despite its bold markings, this shorebird is a fine example of protective coloring. The prominent black band breaks up the plover's outline and makes it virtually invisible against a stony or pebbly background. On beaches where it feeds, its back blends in so well with the wet sand or mud that the bird may escape notice—even at close range—until it moves. The word semi-palmated means "half-webbed" and describes the bird's toes, which are webbed for only about half their length.

◄ **Snowy Plover** (AT LEFT) This pale-colored shorebird, almost unmarked except for an incomplete neckband, lives mostly on beaches above the high-tide line. Though difficult to spot in such surroundings, it sometimes gives itself away by the plover habit of bobbing its head. On Atlantic beaches the Snowy Plover is replaced by the orange-legged Piping Plover (*Charadrius melodus*). Both species lay speckled eggs in shallow "scrapes," which may be lined with bits of shell or other material. Increasing beach traffic is interfering with the nesting of these small plovers.

NONBREEDING

BREEDING

American Golden-plover
Pluvialis dominicus

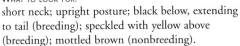

LENGTH:
9-11 in.

WHAT TO LOOK FOR:
short neck; upright posture; black below, extending to tail (breeding); speckled with yellow above (breeding); mottled brown (nonbreeding).

HABITAT:
tundra; mud flats, grasslands (migration).

Once far more common than today, this trim, fast-flying bird was almost wiped out by market gunners. Audubon, watching near New Orleans in 1821, estimated that the 200 gunners standing within his view would bring down 48,000 birds that day. The species may have been saved by its unusual migration route: in late summer and fall, most Golden-plovers fly nonstop over the Atlantic from Nova Scotia to the South American pampas. Returning in spring, they use a different route—north up the Mississippi Valley.

Black-bellied Plover
Pluvialis squatarola

LENGTH:
11-15 in.

WHAT TO LOOK FOR:
black patch under wing; underparts black, except white undertail (breeding); whitish above, with black flecks (breeding); nonbreeding bird grayish.

HABITAT:
tundra; prairies, wetlands (migration); mud flats, salt marshes (winter).

NONBREEDING

BREEDING

Killdeer

Charadrius vociferus

LENGTH:
8½–11 in.

WHAT TO LOOK FOR:
2 black bars across upper chest; white collar, forehead, spot behind eye; reddish rump and upper tail; wide white wing stripe visible in flight.

HABITAT:
prairies, meadows, other open areas, coasts, mud flats, irrigated land.

This familiar plover nests on open ground, not necessarily near water. The nest is at best a depression in the ground, but it is defended valiantly when it contains eggs or young. An approaching grazing animal is the object of a threat display: the bird spreads its wings and tail, scolds, and may even fly at the animal. If a potential predator comes very near, however, the Killdeer tries to lure it away by playing wounded. With one wing held up over the back and the other flapping on the ground, it waits for the intruder to get close, then runs and repeats the display until the intruder is a safe distance from the nest or young. The Killdeer's name echoes its loud, ringing call.

◄ **Black-bellied Plover** (AT LEFT) A shyer bird than the Golden-plover, this species survived the 19th century in greater numbers. Early hunters sometimes wrote admiringly of the Black-bellied Plover's alertness and caution. Its plaintive whistle—*pe-u-eee*—may announce its arrival long before the bird is seen. In marshes and fields it eats grasshoppers, seeds, and berries. But it is more often seen feeding at low tide on mud flats or at the water's edge. Then it will tilt forward to pick up some marine tidbit, run a few steps, and dip again, often pausing with head erect as if listening for danger.

Ruddy Turnstone

Arenaria interpres

LENGTH:
7-9 in.

WHAT TO LOOK FOR:
chunky bird; orange legs; black and white pattern on head and chest; red-brown back (nonbreeder dusky); striking color pattern in flight.

HABITAT:
tundra; coasts (migration, winter).

Turnstones use their bills to get at animal food under stones, as well as under shells and driftwood. An object too heavy for one bird may be rolled aside by two working together. Or a single bird will put its breast against the object and shove. Ruddy Turnstones also dig in drifts of debris along the tide line, tossing bits of seaweed and shells about in what one observer called a perfect shower. In the process, this stocky shorebird may excavate a hole nearly big enough to furnish a place to hide.

Black Turnstone

Arenaria melanocephala

LENGTH:
about 9 in.

WHAT TO LOOK FOR:
blackish gray above and on chest, white below; legs and feet blackish; black and white pattern in flight.

HABITAT:
tundra; rocky coasts (migration, winter).

Unlike the Ruddy Turnstone, which nests in Arctic regions around the world, the Black Turnstone breeds only on the Alaskan coast, where its nest is usually a grass-lined hollow in the mud. Both parents help brood the eggs during the 21-day incubation period. Black Turnstones are the sentinels of the tundra shore. Ever alert, they will pursue even the fiercest predatory birds, uttering high-pitched alarm notes during the chase. When danger threatens the nest, they call sharply *peet, weet, weet*—quite like the call of the familiar Spotted Sandpiper.

NONBREEDING

BREEDING

Red Knot

Calidris canutus

LENGTH:
10-11 in.

WHAT TO LOOK FOR:
plump, short-necked bird; short
bill; breast red-brown (whitish
on nonbreeding bird).

HABITAT:
tundra; tidal flats, beaches
(migration, winter).

*breeds in Alaska and
on Canadian islands*

The word "knot" is thought by some to be linked to the Danish king Canute, who, it was said, liked to eat this kind of bird. Others point out that knots often utter a low, clucking *knut*. Red Knots breed in Arctic regions around the globe and migrate as far south as Australia and South America. They travel in tight formations, often making astonishingly synchronized turns, swoops, and upward dashes. On the flats at low tide they feed in close ranks, plodding along in a businesslike fashion as they probe the mud for food.

NONBREEDING

BREEDING

Long-billed Dowitcher

Limnodromus scolopaceus

LENGTH:
9½–10½ in.

WHAT TO LOOK FOR:
bill long, sturdy, held straight down in feeding; mottled above, with rusty breast (breeding); rump and lower back white; tail white, barred with black.

HABITAT:
tundra; pools, marshes, tidal flats (migration, winter).

Some closely related birds seem designed to confuse people. The two dowitcher species—the Long-billed and the Short-billed (*Limnodromus griseus*)—are such a pair. Even when the two are seen together, the difference in bill length is not easily detected. There is a slight difference in overall size (the Long-billed is larger). And the voices differ: although each species utters a one-syllable note (singly or in a series), the Long-billed's squeaky *keek* contrasts with the low-pitched *tu* of its relative.

Dunlin
Calidris alpina

BREEDING

NONBREEDING

LENGTH:
8-9 in.

WHAT TO LOOK FOR:
black belly (breeding); bill long, drooping at tip; brownish red above (breeding).

HABITAT:
tundra; marshes, ponds, tidal areas (migration, winter).

Sometimes called the Red-backed Sandpiper (a reference to its breeding plumage), this species winters along both coasts. Dunlins feed on wet surfaces, tapping them with slightly open bills. One ornithologist examined a mud flat where Dunlins had recently fed; it was dotted with innumerable shallow dents, "not much larger than those on a thimble," he reported. When the food, often a marine worm, is located, the bird inserts its bill and pulls it out.

NONBREEDING

BREEDING

Sanderling
Calidris alba

LENGTH:
7-8 in.

WHAT TO LOOK FOR:
mottled red head, chest, and back (breeding); gray above, white below (nonbreeding); black legs and bill; wide white wing stripe visible in flight.

HABITAT:
tundra; sandy shores (migration, winter).

The "little one of the sands" is the shorebird most partial to the outer beach. Sanderlings feed right at the margin of the water, where incoming waves drop their load of food. A line of birds will scamper forward, pecking rapidly, eating on the run, then retreating as the next wave approaches. Large flocks may easily be spooked, but small groups will not take wing when a beach walker approaches.

mixed flock of shorebirds

IMMATURE

Least Sandpiper

Calidris minutilla

LENGTH: 5-6 in.

WHAT TO LOOK FOR:
small size; dark brown back (paler on nonbreeding bird); streaked breast; yellow legs; often feeds in grassy and muddy areas.

HABITAT:
tundra, northern wetlands; marshes, ponds, mud flats, tidal areas (migration, winter).

The smallest North American sandpipers are sometimes called mud peeps because of their fondness for oozy tidal flats. Like most other sandpipers, the male of this species performs a courtship flight. He rises with wings bent downward and vibrating, flutters in circles, and trills repeatedly. He may climb as high as 150 feet and often changes altitude during a sustained performance. He also sings from the ground. The songs are variable in sound; one observer noted a particularly lovely series of pure, sweet trills progressing up an octave in a minor key.

Semipalmated Sandpiper

Calidris pusilla

LENGTH: 5-7 in.

WHAT TO LOOK FOR:
mottled grayish brown above (grayer on non-breeding bird), white below; black legs and feet.

HABITAT:
tundra; lakeshores, wetlands, coasts (migration, winter).

Often seen in large flocks with other peeps, the Semipalmated Sandpiper may be the commonest North American shorebird. Its young, like those of most shorebirds, are able to leave the nest within hours of hatching. Pale below and buffy with light markings above, the chicks blend well with their tundra surroundings and literally disappear once they stop toddling along. In Alaska, a Snowy Owl was seen flying toward a female sandpiper and her brood. They flattened and froze. The owl reached the spot, poised above it and then flew on, apparently unable to locate its camouflaged prey.

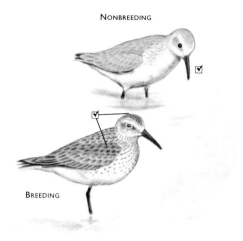

BREEDING

Western Sandpiper

Calidris mauri

LENGTH:
6-7 in.

WHAT TO LOOK FOR:
bill long (especially on female), drooping at tip;
black legs; reddish above, streaked on face and
chest (grayer on nonbreeding bird); often feeds
in deeper water than other small sandpipers.

HABITAT:
tundra; marshes, mud flats, coastal areas
(migration, winter).

The small sandpipers are collectively referred to as peeps. Among them are several that
cannot easily be told apart, especially when the birds are not in breeding plumage. The
different calls are helpful in identification. The Western Sandpiper most often gives a
high, squeaky *cheep* or *chireep*, suggesting the call of a young robin. The Semipalmated
Sandpiper's call is a lower-pitched *krip, cherk,* or *chrruk*. That of the Least Sandpiper is a
soft, high-pitched *breep* or *threep*. Some knowledge of migration routes will also make
identification easier. The Western Sandpiper, for instance, migrates mostly down the
Pacific Coast, where the Semipalmated is extremely rare.

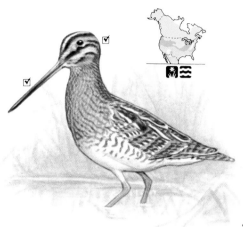

Common Snipe
Gallinago gallinago

LENGTH:
10-12 in.

WHAT TO LOOK FOR:
bill long, slender; head, throat, and back streaked; dark rump; moderately long legs.

HABITAT:
freshwater marshes, swamps, bogs; wet meadows, streamsides.

Snipe and woodcock are technically sandpipers, though in habitat and range they are vastly different from most of their relatives. Snipe are birds of the marshy meadows. The male is famed for his spectacular courtship flights, often performed at dusk in spring. From high above, where the bird may be out of sight, a humming, winnowing sound filters down to earth. This eerie sound is not vocal. It is produced as air is forced through the bird's fanned-out tail feathers during his successive swoops and dives.

American Woodcock
Scolopax minor

LENGTH:
10-12 in.

WHAT TO LOOK FOR:
chunky, short-legged bird; long bill; rounded wings; short tail; wings whistle when bird suddenly takes flight.

HABITAT:
moist woodlands near clearings; alder thickets, wet bottomlands.

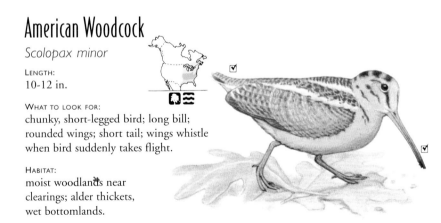

Solitary Sandpiper
Tringa solitaria

LENGTH:
7-9 in.

WHAT TO LOOK FOR:
white eye ring; barred tail; legs long, dark; no white wing stripe.

HABITAT:
forested wetlands, edges of lakes, streams; occasionally in coastal areas (winter).

This slim and elegant bird is an unusual sandpiper: it lays its eggs not on the ground but in old tree nests of such birds as robins and grackles. It feeds in marshes and swamps, on mud flats, along slow-moving brooks, and around ponds and puddles. Although it may be confused with the Spotted Sandpiper, the Solitary Sandpiper is not as restless, teeters much less, and shows no wing stripe when it flies. Its *peet-weet, peet-weet-weet* calls, similar to those of the Spotted Sandpiper, have a thinner, higher quality.

◀ American Woodcock (AT LEFT) The male woodcock's spring courtship display begins with thin, nasal *peenting* at dusk and dawn (sometimes at night). Then the bird takes off, its wings producing a musical flutter as it rises two or three hundred feet in the air. Circling randomly, it begins a bubbly chipping that it continues as it descends. The American Woodcock prefers somewhat drier territory than the Common Snipe, but the two may occur in the same area. At a quick glance they look somewhat alike. A "flushed" woodcock, however, goes off in a straight line instead of zigzagging. Another difference is the barring on the heads, which is crosswise on the woodcock and lengthwise on the snipe.

Pectoral Sandpiper

Calidris melanotos

LENGTH:
8-9 in.

WHAT TO LOOK FOR:
breast buffy, with rows of vertical dashes, sharply separated from white underparts; yellowish legs.

HABITAT:
tundra; wetlands, ponds, meadows, marshes (migration).

These far-ranging shorebirds breed from Alaska east to Hudson Bay and winter in South America. On their trip north, made mostly through the central states, they stop over in marshes and grasslands instead of the mud flats and beaches favored by other sandpipers. This species is likely to stand motionless when alarmed, then take off in a zigzag flight. On the Arctic breeding grounds, displaying males puff out an inflatable sac in their throats and utter deep, resounding booms or hoots.

Wilson's Phalarope
Phalaropus tricolor

LENGTH:
8-10 in.

WHAT TO LOOK FOR:
neck long, slender; thin bill; female
with black and red stripe on neck; male
paler, less reddish; gray above on nonbreeding bird.

HABITAT:
areas with pools of shallow
water, including marshes
and tidal flats.

MALE

FEMALE

Phalaropes are remarkable
birds in several respects.
Although technically shorebirds, they spend much time
swimming in open water.
When they breed, it is the
colorful females that do
the courting and the drab
males that build the nest,
incubate the eggs, and raise
the young. Wilson's Phalarope
is the phalarope most likely to be seen, for it is mainly a freshwater species. It feeds in the
middle of shallow prairie lakes and ponds, spinning around in circles and dabbing for floating
food with its long slender bill. The Red and the Northern Phalaropes (*Phalaropus fulicaria*
and *lobatus*) are more marine.

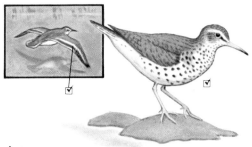

Spotted Sandpiper

Actitis macularia

LENGTH:
7-8 in.

WHAT TO LOOK FOR:
back dark; underside white with
round black spots (breeding); white
wing stripe in flight.

HABITAT:
pebbly edges of rivers, streams,
lakes, ponds; occasionally in coastal
areas (migration, winter).

The nicknames given the Spotted Sandpiper—Tip-up, Teeter-bob, Teeter-tail—point out
the characteristic action by which it can be identified. As the bird moves along, it continually tips forward and backward. When disturbed, it flies low, with wings held at or
below the horizontal. Unlike the typical sandpiper, female "Spotties" are not monoga-
mous: they may mate with two or three males. Only the last male gets help from the
female in incubating the eggs and caring for the young.

Upland Sandpiper

Bartramia longicauda

LENGTH:
9½-10½ in.

WHAT TO LOOK FOR:
small head; long neck; brownish above, white below, with mottled breast and flanks; outer wing feathers much darker than rest of wing and back; central tail feathers dark brown, outer ones barred.

HABITAT:
grasslands, prairies, cultivated fields.

This long-winged bird flies very high on migration and sometimes also during courtship. When it drops to earth it may dive with wings closed and brake only a few feet from the ground. It lands gently and holds its wings open above its back for a moment, then folds them carefully. The Upland Sandpiper's voice can be extremely moving. "Once heard in its perfection it will never be forgotten," promised one ornithologist. The common call is a "sweet, mellow, rolling trill." With some ploverlike habits, this species was once called a sandpiper, then a plover. Recently it has been classified as a sandpiper once again.

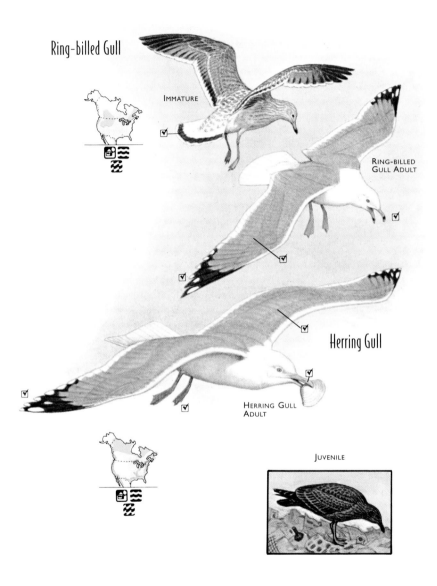

Ring-billed Gull

IMMATURE

RING-BILLED
GULL ADULT

Herring Gull

HERRING GULL
ADULT

JUVENILE

Ring-billed Gull

Larus delawarensis

LENGTH:
17-20 in.

WHAT TO LOOK FOR:
light gray mantle; wing tips black, with white spots; bill yellow, with black ring near tip; yellow legs; immature with narrow black band on tail.

HABITAT:
lakes, rivers, coasts, garbage dumps.

The different kinds of gulls are often difficult to identify. Success depends on sorting out a number of details: relative size; color of the head, of the back and upper wing surface (or mantle), and of the bill and legs; markings on the wing tips and tail. Gulls also undergo both seasonal and growth changes in plumage. Like immature gulls of many other species, young Ring-billed Gulls have a brownish mantle and a mottled head. The adults look like small versions of the more familiar Herring Gull, the California Gull (*Larus californicus*), and various other gulls as well.

Herring Gull

Larus argentatus

LENGTH:
22-26 in.

WHAT TO LOOK FOR:
mantle light gray; wing tips black, with white spots; yellow bill (red spot near tip); pinkish legs; juvenile (very young) and immature bird brownish, with dark tail.

HABITAT:
lakes, rivers, coasts, garbage dumps.

This widespread species plays an important role in cleaning up harbors and beaches. But the Herring Gull is more than a scavenger. It relishes crabs and other marine tidbits, and is well known for cracking clams open by dropping them on rocks and roads. It also preys on the eggs and young of other birds. Herring Gulls nest in colonies, usually in dunes behind the high-tide line. Nests are crude affairs of sticks, seaweed, and other vegetation. The fuzzy, spotted chicks peck at the conspicuous red spot on the adult's bill when they are ready for a meal of regurgitated food.

Great Black-backed Gull

Larus marinus

LENGTH:
27-32 in.

WHAT TO LOOK FOR:
black mantle; bill yellow, with reddish spot near tip;
pink legs; immature with dark bill and narrow
white tip on tail.

HABITAT:
coasts, shores of large lakes and rivers, garbage
dumps.

IMMATURE

Like the Herring Gull,
the world's largest
gull is expanding
its range to the
south. The Great Black-
backed Gull is a scavenger and
predator. In any mixed gathering of gulls, this impressive
bird usually occupies the highest perch, dominating the others and often robbing them of
their food. Another dark-backed
species is the Western Gull (*Larus
occidentalis*). Common along the
Pacific Coast, it is a smaller bird,
with a slate-colored mantle
instead of a black one.

Franklin's Gull

Larus pipixcan

LENGTH:
14-16 in.

WHAT TO LOOK FOR:
all plumages similar to Laughing Gull's, but adult Franklin's
Gull has narrow white band separating gray mantle from
black wing tips.

HABITAT:
prairies, marshes, ponds; coasts (winter).

NONBREEDING ADULT

BREEDING

Although a close relative of the saltwater-loving Laughing
Gull (see page 70), Franklin's Gull breeds far inland, in
prairie marshes. Its floating nest is built of dead reeds and
anchored to growing vegetation. In summer large bands of
these graceful fliers can he seen circling over the grasslands
like pigeons, catching flying insects on the wing. The species
was named for Sir John Franklin, a 19th-century explorer.

Laughing Gull

Larus atricilla

LENGTH:
15-17 in.

WHAT TO LOOK FOR:
small size; head black (breeding) or white with gray nape patch (non-breeding); mantle dark gray; wing tips black; wing with white trailing edge; immature dark above and on breast, with dark band on tail.

HABITAT:
coasts, estuaries, salt marshes.

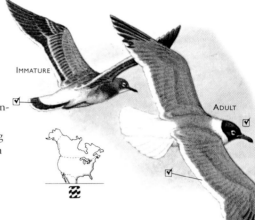

IMMATURE

ADULT

Laughing Gulls are never found far from the coast, though small groups visit fresh-water to bathe and drink. They also visit plowed fields in search of earthworms and insects. In southern waters these gulls keep company with Brown Pelicans and steal fish from their pouches. Laughing Gulls sometimes scavenge in dumps, and frequently they follow fishing boats for refuse and handouts. Their name comes from their hearty but wailing *ha-ha-ha*.

Bonaparte's Gull

Larus philadelphia

winters in Great Lakes

LENGTH:
12-14 in.

WHAT TO LOOK FOR:
small size; black head (nonbreeding white, with black spot behind eye); light gray mantle; white triangle on outer wing; black bill; reddish legs.

HABITAT:
muskeg; coasts, estuaries (winter).

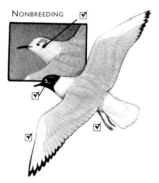

NONBREEDING

Heermann's Gull

Larus heermanni

LENGTH:
17-20 in.

WHAT TO LOOK FOR:
only all-dark gull with lighter head; red bill; immature dark brownish gray.

HABITAT:
coasts, offshore waters (post-breeding, winter).

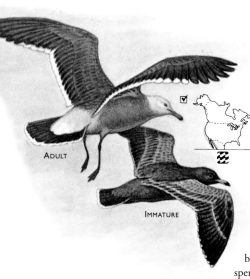

ADULT

IMMATURE

This darkest of gulls is an oddity, not only for its color but for its migratory habits. Heermann's Gulls nest on Mexican islands in spring. After breeding, part of the population spends the summer far to the north, then winters off California. Meanwhile, others migrate south to Guatemala for the summer. Heermann's Gulls, like Laughing Gulls, often rob pelicans of their catch, but they also take their own fish by snapping them up from the surface.

◀ Bonaparte's Gull (AT LEFT) Bonaparte's Gulls breed in boggy, forested areas of the North, where they build stick nests in spruces. Occasionally as high as 20 feet off the ground, the nests are lined with grass and moss. In winter, flocks of Bonaparte's Gulls appear on both coasts. These small gulls fly in a light, bouncy, ternlike fashion and feed on the wing by picking up small fish and crustaceans from the surface of the water. They are named not for the famous emperor Napoleon but for his nephew Charles Lucien Bonaparte, an ornithologist.

NONBREEDING

Forster's Tern

Sterna forsteri

LENGTH:
13½-16 in.

WHAT TO LOOK FOR:
tail deeply forked; mantle gray, with white outer wing; breeding bird with black-tipped reddish-orange bill and black cap; nonbreeding bird with white head, black eye streak, and mostly black bill.

HABITAT:
marshes, lakes, ponds, coasts.

A typical tern in appearance, with its forked tail and long pointed wings, Forster's Tern is not typical in behavior. It is a bird of the marshes, seldom seen on the beaches where many of its relatives breed. Its nest is often a neat grass-lined cup, not a mere scrape in the sand. And it has the unternlike habit of catching insects on the wing. Where several species of terns occur, Forster's can be recognized by its nasal, low-pitched *zrurr, zreep,* or *tza-aap.*

Common Tern

Sterna hirundo

LENGTH:
13-15 in.

WHAT TO LOOK FOR:
tail deeply forked; mantle gray, with some black on outer wing; breeding bird with black-tipped red bill, black cap, and reddish legs and feet; non-breeding bird with white forehead and crown, black eye streak and nape.

HABITAT:
marshes, lakes, coasts.

Terns on the wing are a pleasure to watch. Graceful, buoyant, and swift, Common Terns are a familiar sight hovering over inland lakes, saltwater harbors, and nesting beaches. The breeding range of the similar Arctic Tern (*Sterna paradisaea*) overlaps the Common Tern's in the Northeast, and there the species are easily confused. Even their calls—a penetrating *kee-arr* and *kip-ki-kip*—sound alike.

Black Skimmer

Rynchops niger

LENGTH:
16-18 in.

WHAT TO LOOK FOR:
large size; bill heavy, red, black-tipped, with long lower
mandible; black above, white below; immature mottled
brown above.

HABITAT:
salt marshes, coasts, estuaries, lagoons.

The Cutwater, as this relative of the gulls and terns was once
called, flies along just above the surface, with the tip of its lower
bill held submerged. In this position it skims, or scoops up, small
fish and crustaceans. The lower jaw may be an inch longer than
the upper, and grows about twice as fast because of continual
wearing by the water. Skimmers also feed while wading in the
shallows—dipping for their prey just like "a chick picking up a
worm on dry land," as one observer wrote.

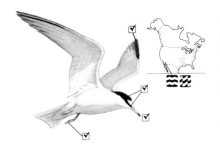

Least Tern

Sterna antillarum

LENGTH:
8-9 in.

WHAT TO LOOK FOR:
small size; tail slightly forked; yellow bill; black cap and eye stripe (breeding); white forehead; mantle gray with black outer wing feathers; feet and legs yellowish.

HABITAT:
mud flats, beaches, rivers, estuaries, coasts.

Like other terns, the smallest North American species usually breeds in colonies. The female lays two or three speckled eggs in a shallow scrape in the sand, sometimes lined with vegetation, pebbles, or bits of shell. The young birds hatch as sand-colored chicks and can fly in their third week. This species has earned the nickname Little Striker because of the way it hovers above the water and plunges for fish.

Black Tern

Chlidonias niger

LENGTH:
8½-10 in.

WHAT TO LOOK FOR:
small size; appears very dark in flight; head and belly black (some white on nonbreeding birds); dark gray mantle, rump, and tail.

HABITAT:
lakes, ponds, marshes; coasts (migration).

Though the Black Tern is frequently seen along the coast, it breeds on inland lakes and in freshwater or brackish marshes. The nest is built in a slightly elevated situation surrounded by water, such as the top of a muskrat house. The other dark-backed species likely to be seen in North American waters are the Sooty Tern (*Sterna fuscata*) and the Brown Noddy (*Anous stolidus*), which breed in the Dry Tortugas, southwest of the Florida Keys.

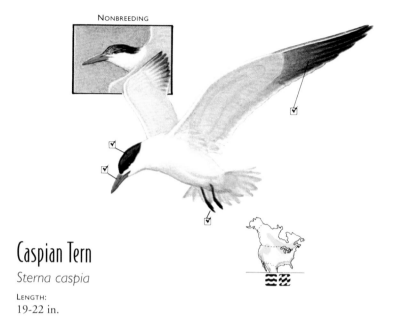

NONBREEDING

Caspian Tern

Sterna caspia

LENGTH:
19-22 in.

WHAT TO LOOK FOR:
large size; heavy red bill; black cap (forehead streaked with white on nonbreeding bird); mantle gray; outer wings blackish on underside; black legs and feet.

HABITAT:
lakes, marshes, estuaries, coasts.

The Caspian Tern is almost as big as a Herring Gull, and with its soaring flight, it behaves like one. It breeds around the world, nesting along the shores of lakes and oceans; the first description of the species was based on a specimen collected on the Caspian Sea. The Royal Tern (*Sterna maxima*), of our southern coasts, is almost as large, but has a thinner orange-yellow bill, shorter legs, and at most times a white forehead.

Common Murre

Uria aalge

LENGTH:
14-16 in.

WHAT TO LOOK FOR:
black above, white below; bill
long, thin; nonbreeding bird
with more white on head; usually
seen offshore when not breeding.

HABITAT:
rocky coasts, islands, islets; open
seas (winter).

Common Murres breed in large colonies on ocean cliffs. The female lays a single
pear-shaped egg on bare rock (the shape makes it less likely that the egg will roll
off a narrow ledge). Before the young can fly, they leave the cliff—by plunging
into the sea. In the water they join up with adults (not necessarily their parents),
who feed them for several weeks. Murres fish while swimming underwater, and
each year many thousands are accidentally killed in commercial fishing nets.

TUFTED
PUFFIN

Atlantic Puffin

Fratercula arctica

LENGTH:
10-13 in.

WHAT TO LOOK FOR:
bill large, colorful, flattened at sides; black above, with white face and breast; nonbreeding bird with blackish face and smaller bill; flies with rapid wingbeats.

HABITAT:
rocky coasts; open seas (winter).

The clown of the Atlantic chases fish by literally flying after them underwater. In the nesting season an adult may bring back to its burrow more than 20 small fish in a single beakful. Young puffins are fed by their parents in their burrows for as long as 50 days; after that, they feed themselves at sea. In the Pacific the Tufted Puffin (*Lunda cirrhata*) breeds on islands from southern California north to Alaska.

Turkey Vulture
Cathartes aura

SIZE:
length, 26-32 in.; wingspan, 6 ft.

WHAT TO LOOK FOR:
large black bird; bare red head (blackish on immature); long tail; holds wings in V when soaring.

HABITAT:
various land habitats, especially around dead trees.

Turkey Buzzards, as old-timers call them, are magnificent fliers. Alone or by the dozen, they sail for hours high in the sky, rocking slightly from side to side and holding their wings in a shallow V. The Black Vulture (*Coragyps atratus*), a more southern species, holds its wings flat and flaps them frequently; the Turkey Vulture flaps mainly when seeking updrafts at low altitudes. Vultures eat some live prey, but most of their food is carrion. The largest vulture in North America, the endangered California Condor (*Gymnogyps californianus*), has a 10-foot wingspan.

Sharp-shinned Hawk
Accipiter striatus

LENGTH:
10-14 in.

WHAT TO LOOK FOR:
small size; wings short, rounded; tail long, barred; breast finely striped with cinnamon.

HABITAT:
woodlands, brushy areas.

Red-tailed Hawk

Buteo jamaicensis

SIZE:
length, 19-26 in.;
wingspan, 4½ ft.

WHAT TO LOOK FOR:
bright rufous tail, conspicuous in flight; throat and underparts white, usually with dark belly band; immature with fine barring on brown tail.

HABITAT:
all types of land habitats, especially open woodlands.

The distant, soaring buteo that holds its position in a stiff breeze as if "pinned to the sky" is a Red-tailed Hawk. Plumage variations within this species are great; some western birds, for example, are extremely dark; others are very pale. Red-tails hunt from the air and from exposed perches, such as the tops of dead trees. The bulk of their diet is small mammals. Other large buteos include the less common Ferruginous Hawk (*Buteo regalis*) of western grasslands and the Rough-legged Hawk (*Buteo lagopus*), an Arctic breeder.

◀ Sharp-shinned Hawk (AT LEFT) This is the smallest of the North American accipiters, the dashing hawks that prey on birds and small mammals. Female accipiters are larger than the males. The largest species is the Goshawk (*Accipiter gentilis*) of the northern forests. Cooper's Hawk (*Accipiter cooperii*) resembles the Sharp-shinned Hawk but is a heavier, more deliberate flier. Accipiters fly by flapping their wings a few times, then gliding with wings flat or slightly bowed, then flapping a few more times.

Red-shouldered Hawk

Buteo lineatus

SIZE:
length, 17-24 in.; wingspan, 3½ ft.

WHAT TO LOOK FOR:
reddish-brown shoulder patch;
rufous below, including underwings near body; tail long, with
wide black and narrow white bars;
immature lacking patch, streaked
with brown below.

HABITAT:
moist open forests, bottomlands, other wet areas.

This strikingly marked species is not so conspicuous in its
behavior as the Red-tailed Hawk: it soars less frequently and usually
perches below the treetops. The nest is built in a big tree, most often in a
substantial crotch. The female lays two or three eggs—occasionally more. Incubation
lasts about three and a half weeks, with both parents sharing the job (they also raise the chicks
together). Five or six weeks after hatching, the young leave the nest. Red-shouldered Hawks
eat a wide variety of prey—small mammals, birds, frogs, snakes, lizards, snails, and insects.

Broad-winged Hawk

Buteo platypterus

LENGTH:
13½-19 in.

WHAT TO LOOK FOR:
tail broadly barred with black and white;
wings mostly whitish below; breast with
brownish-red bars; immature with streaks on
underside and more finely barred tail.

HABITAT:
deciduous forests.

Swainson's Hawk

Buteo swainsoni

LENGTH:
19-22 in.

WHAT TO LOOK FOR:
tail finely barred, with
broad band near tip; dark above; underside
all dark (dark phase) or mostly
white with dark breast band
(light phase); immature with
heavily streaked breast.

HABITAT:
brushlands, plains, open
forests, foothills.

A western species common on the
Great Plains, Swainson's Hawk
travels in groups on migration, as
does the Broad-winged Hawk. In flight it
holds its wings slightly above the horizontal—a useful identification clue. When a migrating
group settles to roost for the night, some of them will rest on the ground if there is a short-
age of tree perches. They often feed on the ground as well, hopping after crickets and
grasshoppers. They catch gophers by perching on hillocks of earth in front of the rodents'
burrows and waiting for an unwary individual to appear.

◀ Broad-winged Hawk (AT LEFT) This forest-loving buteo is quiet, almost sedentary in
behavior. But in the breeding season the pairs are conspicuous as they soar overhead, whistling *p' deeee, p' deeee.* Their migration is spectacular. The birds proceed
by spiraling up on a thermal—a column of warmed, rising air—and then gliding
on to the next. As they go, they collect in large groups (kettles) that string out in
long lines between thermals, often too high to be seen by the naked eye.

Golden Eagle
Aquila chrysaetos

SIZE:
length, 30-41 in.; wingspan, to 7½ ft.

WHAT TO LOOK FOR:
large size; wings held level when soaring; dark brown with golden-brown crown and nape; immature with white at base of tail and flight feathers.

HABITAT:
remote open areas, mountains, forests.

Golden Eagles are magnificent fliers and dashing hunters. Fast enough to take grouse and ptarmigan on the wing, they usually prey on ground squirrels, prairie dogs, and rabbits. They will attack mammals up to the size of deer, especially in winter, though they cannot carry off the heavier animals. Golden Eagles build large stick nests on rock ledges or in trees and have been known to defend breeding territories of up to 75 square miles. The young birds, with conspicuous white areas on their wings and tail, look very different from the adults.

Osprey
Pandion haliaetus

SIZE:
length, 21-25 in.; wingspan, to 6 ft.

WHAT TO LOOK FOR:
white head, with dark stripe through eye; brown above, mostly white below; wings long, crooked in flight, with dark patch below at bend.

HABITAT:
usually near large bodies of water.

Bald Eagle

Haliaeetus leucocephalus

SIZE:
length, 35-40 in.;
wingspan, to 7½ ft.

WHAT TO LOOK FOR:
large size; head, neck, and tail
white; rest of plumage dark
brown; immature brown, with
whitish wing linings.

HABITAT:
open areas, forests, near water.

This bird is "bald" not because its
head is featherless but because the
head of the adult is white—an old meaning of the word. Bald Eagles probably
mate for life. They build a nest in a
tree, on a cliff, or even on the ground
and add to it each year, using such materi-
als as sticks, weeds, and earth, until it may weigh a thousand
pounds or more. One observer saw a bird lift and fly away with
the top of a muskrat house—presumably as a handy package of nest
makings. Bald Eagles eat carrion, waterfowl, and especially fish. Past
declines caused by pesticides have been reversed due to environmental
cleanups and programs of re-introduction of eagles.

◀ Osprey (AT LEFT) The Osprey, or Fish Hawk, sights its prey while hovering, then
plunges feetfirst into the water. Sharp talons pierce and lock into the fish; when the
bird rises, it is almost always carrying its catch headfirst. Ospreys nest on dead trees,
floating buoys, utility poles and towers, and rarely (if undisturbed) on the ground.
The stick nest may contain rope and miscellaneous debris that has washed up on
shore, as well as sprigs of greenery—a characteristic also common to hawk and eagle
nests. In recent years the Osprey has begun to recover from the disastrous effects of
pesticides and other pollutants.

Northern Harrier

Circus cyaneus

LENGTH:
17-24 in.

WHAT TO LOOK FOR:
long wings and tail; white rump; male gray above, white below; female and immature dark brown above, lighter below.

HABITAT:
prairies, open areas, all types of marshes.

FEMALE

This species, formerly called the Marsh Hawk, is a relentless hunter. With its long wings held up in a slight V, it pursues—or "harries"—its quarry, zigzagging low over field or marsh. On nesting territory the gray male dives and climbs, dives and climbs, in what one watcher likened to a series of capital U's. Or he may tumble from high up. When he brings food to his brown mate on the ground nest, she flies up, he drops his prey, and she catches it in midair—or they may make the exchange claw to claw, without his alighting.

American Kestrel

Falco sparverius

LENGTH: 9-12 in.

WHAT TO LOOK FOR: small size; male rufous, with blue-gray wings, dark facial pattern, and black band near tip of tail; female with rufous wings and blackish bars on rufous back and tail; hovering behavior.

HABITAT: open wooded areas, prairies, deserts, farmlands, suburbs, cities.

FEMALE

MALE

This adaptable little falcon is regularly seen hunting along parkways and in suburban fields. It has two hunting techniques. It may wait on a treetop, pole, or telephone wire until it sights its prey; then it takes off in a dive or glide. Or it may fly out over a field and hover on fast-beating wings before it drops. The American Kestrel used to be called the Sparrow Hawk. It does eat birds, but takes many more insects and small mammals.

Peregrine Falcon

Falco peregrinus

LENGTH:
15-20 in.

WHAT TO LOOK FOR:
pointed wings; long tail; bluish gray above, with blackish "mustache" and finely barred whitish breast; immature brown above, with brown "mustache" and brown streaks below.

HABITAT:
open areas from mountains to coasts.

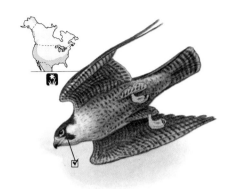

In North America this worldwide species used to be called the Duck Hawk. Fully capable of taking ducks and other water birds, the Peregrine is an extremely fast flier (one individual was clocked in a dive at 275 miles an hour). In the eastern United States the Peregrine has been wiped out as a breeding species by a combination of pesticides and human disturbance. Now, however, a novel restocking project aims at creating a new population of wild birds.

Prairie Falcon

Falco mexicanus

LENGTH: 17-20 in.

WHAT TO LOOK FOR: pointed wings; long tail; light brown above, with head pattern; whitish below, with dark streaks on underside and black patch at base of wings.

HABITAT: open areas in mountains, prairies, deserts.

Falcons have been admired through the centuries for their powers of flight. The large species, like the Prairie Falcon, prey mostly on birds, which they sometimes pick out of the air in spectacular dives, striking with extended talons. Like most members of its family, this species is not much of a nest builder. The female, somewhat bigger than the male but similar in appearance, lays her eggs on top of a high, isolated rock or on a cliff ledge; or she may take over the abandoned nest of another bird, commonly a raven.

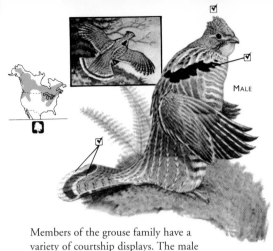

Ruffed Grouse

Bonasa umbellus

MALE

LENGTH:
16–19 in.

WHAT TO LOOK FOR:
small crest; blackish ruff (shorter on female); tail fan-shaped when spread, edged with white and black; mottled brown, gray, or reddish above.

HABITAT:
mixed or deciduous forests.

Members of the grouse family have a variety of courtship displays. The male Ruffed Grouse stands on a log and drums the air with his wings, slowly at first, then fast, producing a soft, far-carrying *thump, thump, thump-ump-ump-prrrr*. The Spruce Grouse (*Dendragapus canadensis*) of northern forests drums during short flights. The Blue Grouse (*Dendragapus obscurus*) of the western mountains produces booming notes with the colorful air sacs on his neck.

WINTER

MALE

White-tailed Ptarmigan

Lagopus leucurus

LENGTH:
12–13 in.

WHAT TO LOOK FOR:
mottled brown, with tail, belly, and most of wings white; all white in winter; red patch over eye.

HABITAT:
mountains above timberline, alpine meadows; lower elevations (winter).

The source of the word *ptarmigan* is unknown. One authority suggests that it may come from a Gaelic word meaning "mountaineer." The White-tailed Ptarmigan certainly fits that description, for the hardy bird seldom descends to the tree line. Feathered feet help it conserve heat, and it can survive the winter by feeding on nothing more than willow buds. In the breeding season the female's subtly mottled plumage camouflages her on the nest; in winter both sexes match the snowy background.

Sharp-tailed Grouse

Tympanuchus phasianellus

LENGTH:
14-20 in.

WHAT TO LOOK FOR:
tail narrow, pointed, showing white on outer feathers in flight; tawny brown above, with darker barring; lighter below, with chevron markings.

HABITAT:
prairies, brushy areas.

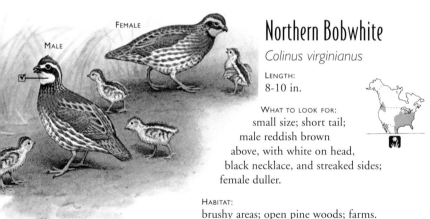

MALE DISPLAYING

Traditional dancing grounds are the setting for the courtship of the Sharp-tailed Grouse. Early on spring mornings the cocks gather. They droop their wings, erect their tails, puff themselves up, and inflate the colorful air sacs on their necks. Then they stamp, run, and leap in a frenzied group dance, competing for dominance and the attention of the hens. Another spectacular dancer is the black-bellied Sage Grouse (*Centrocercus urophasianus*) of western areas.

FEMALE

MALE

Northern Bobwhite

Colinus virginianus

LENGTH:
8-10 in.

WHAT TO LOOK FOR:
small size; short tail; male reddish brown above, with white on head, black necklace, and streaked sides; female duller.

HABITAT:
brushy areas; open pine woods; farms.

Both male and female bobwhites help build the nest—sometimes simply a hollow tramped down in a clump of tall grass, but usually a woven cover of pine needles, grass, and nearby vegetation, with an opening on one side. At night a covey of bobwhite roost on the ground in a circle, with heads outward and bodies touching. This arrangement keeps them warm even when they are covered with snow.

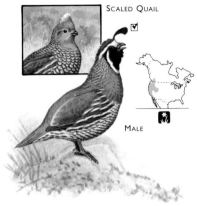

SCALED QUAIL

MALE

California Quail
Callipepla californica

LENGTH:
9-11 in.

WHAT TO LOOK FOR:
forward-curving plume; back brown, breast gray-blue, sides streaked with white; scaly pattern on belly; male with black and white facial pattern.

HABITAT:
brushy areas, meadows, suburbs.

Coveys of plumed California Quail post sentries as they feed. Although they are not shy, they are easily frightened. When they dash for cover, they are more likely to run than fly. Gambel's Quail (*Callipepla gambelii*), a desert bird, also wears a plume. Another dry-area species, the Scaled Quail (*Callipepla squamata*), is nicknamed Cottontop for its white crest.

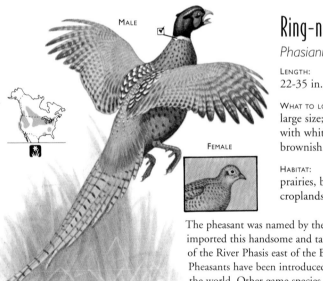

MALE

FEMALE

Ring-necked Pheasant
Phasianus colchicus

LENGTH:
22-35 in.

WHAT TO LOOK FOR:
large size; tail long, pointed; male with white collar; female smaller, brownish.

HABITAT:
prairies, brushy areas, fertile croplands.

The pheasant was named by the ancient Greeks, who imported this handsome and tasty bird from the region of the River Phasis east of the Black Sea. Ring-necked Pheasants have been introduced into the wild around the world. Other game species introduced into North America are the Chukar (*Alectoris chukar*), a large partridge established in the West, and the Gray Partridge (*Perdix perdix*), found here and there across southern Canada and the northern states.

Wild Turkey

Meleagris gallopavo

LENGTH:
3-4 ft.

WHAT TO LOOK FOR:
very large size; tail long, with black band near tip; male glossy brown, with bare, pale bluish head and red wattles; female smaller, duller.

HABITAT:
oak and mesquite brush, deciduous woodlands, wooded bottomlands.

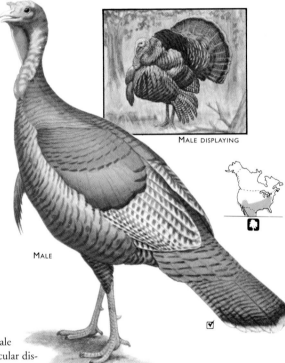

MALE DISPLAYING

MALE

In the breeding period, the male Wild Turkey puts on a spectacular display. He spreads his tail, swells out his wattles, and rattles his wings, gobbling and strutting the whole time. Wiped out in many areas by land development and unrestricted hunting, the species is making a comeback with the help of reintroductions and good management. Turkeys roost in trees and feed on the ground on insects, berries, seeds, and nuts. The hens nest in leaf-lined hollows in brush or woodlands; they alone incubate the eggs, sometimes as many as 20 in a clutch. Wary and difficult to approach, turkeys can fly well for short distances but prefer to walk or run.

Rock Dove (Pigeon)

Columba livia

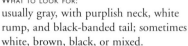

LENGTH:
11-14 in.

WHAT TO LOOK FOR:
usually gray, with purplish neck, white rump, and black-banded tail; sometimes white, brown, black, or mixed.

HABITAT:
cities, towns, farms.

The Rock Dove, originally from Europe and Asia, nests on cliffs in the wild and has easily adapted to the ledges of human buildings. Rock Doves breed several times a year, beginning in March, when the males' ardent cooing is one of the sounds of spring. A mated pair shares the incubation and care of the young, which are fed on regurgitated "pigeon's milk," a secretion from the bird's crop. Breeders have developed several color strains, but free-living flocks usually contain many gray birds with iridescent necks, similar to the original wild Rock Doves.

White-winged Dove

Zenaida asiatica

LENGTH:
10-12 in.

WHAT TO LOOK FOR:
mostly brown; tail rounded; large white patches on wings and outer tail feathers.

HABITAT:
wooded river edges; thickets; brush near water; desert oases; farmlands; towns; cities.

There are a number of species that beginners may overlook because they resemble Rock Doves. The White-winged Dove is one of them. But this bird of the Southwest. the southern Gulf Coast, and points south is somewhat smaller than the familiar city Pigeon and has white at the corners of its tail. The White-winged Dove nests in shrubs, thickets, and trees, usually at a moderate height and often in colonies. The call is a prolonged series of rough hoots; though not particularly loud, the sound carries over long distances.

Mourning Dove

Zenaida macroura

LENGTH: 10-12 in.

WHAT TO LOOK FOR: slim body; tail long, pointed, edged with white; grayish brown above, with scattered black spots.

HABITAT: deserts, brushy areas, woodlands, farmlands, suburbs, parks.

The Mourning Dove's mellow, vaguely melancholy call—*coo-ah, coo, coo, coo*—is repeated again and again, sliding upward on the second syllable and then down for the last three notes. Mourning Doves build a flimsy nest of sticks, usually in an evergreen tree close to the trunk. Two eggs make a set. The parents share incubating duties, the male sitting much of the day and his mate during the night. The young are fed by regurgitation, then gradually weaned to insects and the adults' main food, seeds.

Common Ground-dove

Columbina passerina

LENGTH:
5-6½ in.

WHAT TO LOOK FOR:
small size; tail short, rounded; wings with brownish-red patches visible in flight.

HABITAT:
deserts, dry grasslands, open woodlands, farmlands.

The plump little Common Ground-dove is the smallest of our doves, about the size of a House Sparrow. As it walks along, hunting for seeds, it nods its head (as do other members of its family). This is a tame species and will permit a close approach. Usually it flies for only a short distance, showing bright reddish-brown patches on its wings. In its southern habitat the Ground-dove favors sandy or weedy areas, cotton fields, and citrus groves. The southwestern Inca Dove (*Columbina inca*) somewhat resembles the Ground-dove but has a long, narrow tail edged with white, like that of a Mourning Dove.

Yellow-billed Cuckoo

Coccyzus americanus

LENGTH:
10½-12½ in.

WHAT TO LOOK FOR:
long, slim bird; gray-brown above, white below; underside of tail black, with 3 pairs of large white spots; yellow lower mandible; reddish-brown wing patches visible in flight.

HABITAT:
moist second-growth woodlands; brushy areas near water.

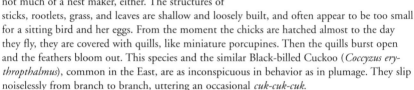

Unlike some cuckoos, the Yellow-billed does not regularly lay its eggs in other birds' nests—but it is not much of a nest maker, either. The structures of sticks, rootlets, grass, and leaves are shallow and loosely built, and often appear to be too small for a sitting bird and her eggs. From the moment the chicks are hatched almost to the day they fly, they are covered with quills, like miniature porcupines. Then the quills burst open and the feathers bloom out. This species and the similar Black-billed Cuckoo (*Coccyzus erythropthalmus*), common in the East, are as inconspicuous in behavior as in plumage. They slip noiselessly from branch to branch, uttering an occasional *cuk-cuk-cuk*.

Belted Kingfisher

Ceryle alcyon

LENGTH:
11-14 in.

WHAT TO LOOK FOR:
shaggy crest; bill heavy, sharp-pointed; blue-gray above, with blue-gray breast band (additional chestnut band on female).

HABITAT:
shores of lakes, ponds, streams; coasts.

FEMALE

MALE

Greater Roadrunner

Geococcyx californianus

LENGTH:
20-24 in.

WHAT TO LOOK FOR:
large size; long tail; rough crest; patch of red and pale blue behind eye; runs rapidly but seldom flies.

HABITAT:
deserts, semiarid areas with scattered brush and trees.

The roadrunner is really a large ground-dwelling cuckoo, although it neither looks nor behaves like a cuckoo. This long-tailed, long-legged bird is very agile and fast on its feet; one was clocked at 15 miles an hour. The roadrunner is known to feed on snakes—poisonous or otherwise—and lizards. It also eats scorpions, spiders, grasshoppers, crickets, small mammals, birds' eggs, and even small birds that it catches in flight by leaping into the air and snatching them with its bill. Most items are simply swallowed, but a big lizard, for instance, is softened by being beaten on a rock. The roadrunner is not a quiet bird. It crows and chuckles. It rolls its mandibles together, producing a clacking sound. And mostly it coos like a dove—a most unusual cuckoo altogether.

◀ **Belted Kingfisher** (AT LEFT) As it leaves a favored perch over-looking a pool or lake, the Belted Kingfisher often utters its rattling call. Still calling, it dashes over the water, keeping its head slightly raised as if it were trying to see just a bit far-ther. It may fish by swooping close to the surface, dipping for its prey. Or it may climb to a considerable height, hold there on beating wings with head cocked, and then plunge. Kingfishers usually nest in a burrow in a steep bank, prefer-ably near water. The tunnel may be as long as 15 feet, end-ing in a slightly elevated nest chamber.

Common Barn-owl

Tyto alba

LENGTH:
13-19 in.

WHAT TO LOOK FOR:
face heart-shaped, mostly white; golden
brown above, usually white below; legs long,
feathered; mothlike flight.

HABITAT:
forests near open country; farmlands, towns.

Long before this worldwide species was a "barn" owl, it nested in hollow trees, caves, and burrows. Often it still does. But man's structures furnish it with ideal cover, and the bird can be found in belfries, attics, and abandoned mines as well as barns. This owl is a nocturnal hunter. Experiments have shown that it requires only its ears to locate prey.

Snowy Owl

Nyctea scandiaca

LENGTH:
19-25 in.

WHAT TO LOOK FOR:
large size; mostly white, with dark flecks; active in daylight.

HABITAT:
tundra; prairies, open fields, marshes, beaches (winter).

Snowy Owls nest on the tundra around the top of the globe. In winters when food (chiefly lemmings and hares) is scarce, large numbers move south to the northern United States. Snowy Owls show little fear of human activities, and so it is not uncommon to see one perched on the roof of a building or on a highway sign beside an airport. The owls are usually silent in winter, but on their breeding grounds they hoot, whistle, rattle, and bark.

Great Horned Owl

Bubo virginianus

LENGTH:
18-24 in.

WHAT TO LOOK FOR:
large size; widely spaced ear tufts; mottled brown above, lighter below, with fine dark barring.

HABITAT:
scrub areas, woodlands, deserts, canyons, bottomlands.

This daring and adaptable species, found virtually throughout the Americas, will attack any medium-sized mammal or bird—porcupine or skunk, duck or grouse. In North America the Great Horned Owl begins to breed in the cold of winter. Two or three eggs are laid, usually in the old nest of a large hawk or crow, sometimes in a hollow tree or a cave. Calls are many and various, but the common one is a series of muffled hoots—*hoo, hoo-hoo, hoooo-hoo.* The male's voice is higher-pitched than the female's, and a pair in concert seem to harmonize, often in thirds.

Northern Pygmy-owl

Glaucidium gnoma

"eye" patch

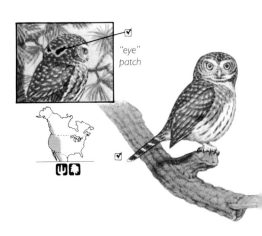

LENGTH:
6-7 in.

WHAT TO LOOK FOR:
very small; brownish above, with white-edged black spots on nape; white below, with dark streaks; tail long, barred with white.

HABITAT:
coniferous and mixed forests; wooded canyons in dry areas.

Barred Owl

Strix varia

LENGTH:
16-23 in.

WHAT TO LOOK FOR:
large round head; no ear tufts; dark eyes; mottled brown, with barred throat and streaked underparts.

HABITAT:
wet woodlands, wooded swamps, floodplains.

In the daytime an owl sitting inconspicuously in a tree is frequently mobbed by a noisy flock of scolding small birds—a sure tip-off to an owl watcher. The Barred Owl's far-carrying, rhythmic hooting, heard by day as well as night, is often written as *Who cooks for you? Who cooks for you-all?* The bird also gives a hair-raising catlike scream. The Barred Owl's larger and rarer relative, the Great Gray Owl (*Strix nebulosa*), breeds in northern and mountain forests but occasionally appears farther south and east during the winter.

◄ Northern Pygmy-owl (AT LEFT) The Northern Pygmy-owl is tiny indeed—no bigger than a good-sized sparrow. It has two distinctive features: a long tail, which it often cocks up at an angle, and two black blotches, or "eyes," on the back of its neck. The species nests in tree holes, usually in evergreen forests. The Ferruginous Pygmy-owl (*Glaucidium brasilianum*), a bird of the southwestern deserts, is similar but is usually more rusty, and always has rusty or buffy bars on its tail. The Elf Owl (*Micrathene whitneyi*) of the Southwest is even tinier and very short-tailed.

LONG-EARED OWL

Short-eared Owl

Asio flammeus

LENGTH:
12-16 in.

WHAT TO LOOK FOR:
head rounded; dark areas on wing; mottled yellowish brown; flight erratic, flapping.

HABITAT:
tundra, brushy areas, prairies, dunes, marshes.

This is a bird of the open country. A daytime and twilight hunter, the Short-eared Owl will occasionally perch on a fence post to spot its rodent prey, but usually it is seen coursing over a pasture or marsh. The range of the Short-eared Owl includes much of the Americas and Eurasia. The Long-eared Owl (*Asio otus*) has a similarly wide range. It is nocturnal, however, and nests in trees, not on the ground.

Burrowing Owl

Speotyto cunicularia

LENGTH:
8-10½ in.

WHAT TO LOOK FOR:
round head; long legs; short tail; brown above, spotted with buff and white; paler below.

HABITAT:
prairies, plains, deserts, other open spaces.

Eastern Screech-owl

Otus asio

LENGTH:
7-10 in.

WHAT TO LOOK FOR:
small size; ear tufts;
reddish, brown, or
gray; sometimes perches in tree holes.

HABITAT:
forests, groves, farmlands, towns, parks.

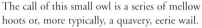

GRAY
PHASE

REDDISH
PHASE

The call of this small owl is a series of mellow
hoots or, more typically, a quavery, eerie wail.
The Screech Owl's wail is not difficult for man to imitate, and such imitations may
get dozens of curious or outraged small birds to respond. The Western Screech-owl
(*Otus kennicottii*), of the western half of the continent, is almost identical, but its
call is a series of soft notes, all on one pitch and speeding up at the end.

◀ Burrowing Owl (AT LEFT) Typically this owl is seen standing at
the entrance to its burrow, bowing and bobbing in a comic
way. In the West it nests in the abandoned burrows of prairie
dogs. A burrow ordinarily slopes down for about 3 feet, then
runs back horizontally to a nesting chamber 10 feet or more
from the entrance. The birds line this chamber with feathers,
grass, dried mammal dung, and the remains of prey. Five or
six eggs make up the set, and both parents incubate and raise
the young. These owls feed on insects, reptiles, and rodents,
hunting during the day as well as in the evening.

Whip-poor-will

Caprimulgus vociferus

LENGTH:
9-10 in.

WHAT TO LOOK FOR:
mottled brown; rounded wings;
white or buff band on throat; white
at end of outer tail feathers (male);
most active at dusk.

HABITAT:
deciduous and mixed woods with clearings.

The Whip-poor-will calls its name continually and emphatically from a
perch in the dark, but its sound seldom gives away its location. The elusive night bird is equally difficult to locate during the day, when it sleeps among the dried leaves of the woodland floor. The female lays two eggs on the ground, without any nest. The Chuck-will's-widow (*Caprimulgus carolinensis*) is common over much of its relative's range and has a similar call, given at a slower tempo. Both eat moths and other nocturnal insects.

Chimney Swift

Chaetura pelagica

LENGTH:
4-5 in.

WHAT TO LOOK FOR:
small size; dark gray, lighter
on throat; bow-shaped wings;
short tail; body looks cigar-
shaped in flight.

HABITAT:
open air over woodlands,
farmlands, towns, cities.

Until man provided chimneys, wells, and other alternative sites, this dark little bird nested in hollow trees. Chimney Swifts pass much of their lives in flight, beating their wings rapidly or holding them stiffly as they sail. They utter a distinctive series of high-pitched chips. No one knew where Chimney Swifts wintered until quite recently, when it was discovered that the entire population migrates to a remote part of the upper Amazon.

Common Nighthawk

Chordeiles minor

LENGTH:
8-10 in.

WHAT TO LOOK FOR:
mottled brown; white areas on throat, wings, and tail (female with buff throat and no tail band); wings long, pointed; tail slightly forked; bouncing flight.

HABITAT:
grasslands, open woods, towns, cities.

Like the Whip-poor-will and others of the family, the Common Nighthawk has a very large mouth, used to capture insects as it flies. The bird does much of its hunting at dusk or in the night, and it calls often in flight (a nasal *beent*). The female lays her eggs on gravel, rock, burned-over ground, or other barren terrain; graveled roofs in urban areas are favorite nesting sites.

White-throated Swift

Aeronautes saxatalis

LENGTH:
6-7 in.

WHAT TO LOOK FOR:
black and white pattern on underside; long wings; notched tail.

HABITAT:
open air over rocky areas, especially canyons and mountains.

The fast-flying "rock swift" of the western mountains roosts and nests in crevices of cliffs, especially those overlooking deep canyons. A single crevice may contain a number of roosting swifts; at sunset a procession will stream in and disappear into the face of the cliff with incredible accuracy and speed. Vaux's Swift (*Chaetura vauxi*), another western species, is smaller than the White-throated, with a grayish breast and shorter, unnotched tail.

Anna's Hummingbird

Calypte anna

LENGTH:
3-4 in.

WHAT TO LOOK FOR:
bill long, slender; metallic green above; iridescent dark red crown and throat (male); white-tipped tail (female).

HABITAT:
open woodlands; chaparral; suburban and city gardens.

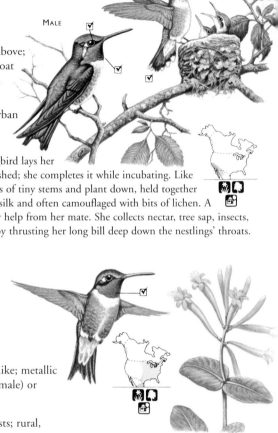

When the female Anna's Hummingbird lays her eggs, her nest may be only half finished; she completes it while incubating. Like most hummingbird nests, it consists of tiny stems and plant down, held together and lashed to a branch with spider silk and often camouflaged with bits of lichen. A female feeds her young without any help from her mate. She collects nectar, tree sap, insects, and spiders, and delivers the meal by thrusting her long bill deep down the nestlings' throats.

Ruby-throated Hummingbird

Archilochus colubris

LENGTH: 3-3½ in.

WHAT TO LOOK FOR: bill long, needlelike; metallic green above; throat metallic red (male) or dingy white (female).

HABITAT: deciduous and mixed forests; rural, suburban, and city gardens.

Of the 15 species of hummingbird that regularly nest north of Mexico, this is the only one breeding east of the Great Plains. The Broad-tailed Hummingbird (*Selasphorus platycercus*) of western mountains is similar in appearance, but the ranges of the two do not overlap. "Hummers," unlike other birds, can fly backwards or straight up and down. They can also hover, and are able to drink flower nectar without actually landing on the blossom. The flowers they drink from are usually long, tubular, and orange or red.

Rufous Hummingbird

Selasphorus rufus

LENGTH:
3½-4 in.

WHAT TO LOOK FOR:
male mostly red-brown, with iridescent orange-red throat and sides of head; female with green back, rufous on flanks and base of tail feathers.

HABITAT:
alpine meadows, edges of woodlands; lowlands (migration).

The Rufous Hummingbird flies farther north than any other hummingbird. As the birds move south toward Mexico (mainly in July and August) they may be found as high in the mountains as 13,200 feet. Hummingbirds are generally feisty, but this species is particularly pugnacious. Yet at times Rufous Hummingbirds appear to breed in colonies, with some pairs nesting only a few feet from one another. The similar-looking Allen's Hummingbird (*Selasphorus sasin*), which occurs along the West Coast from Oregon south, has a green back and cap.

Black-chinned Hummingbird

Archilochus alexandri

LENGTH:
3-3¾ in.

WHAT TO LOOK FOR:
back metallic green; throat black, bordered with iridescent purple (male); slightly forked tail.

HABITAT:
dry scrub, woodlands near streams, wooded canyons, mountain meadows, gardens.

Hummingbirds are unique to the New World. European explorers were astounded by the tiny glittering creatures that zipped up and down, backwards and sideways, with wings humming and blurred. Hummingbirds perform set figures in courtship flights. The male Black-chinned Hummingbird, for instance, swings in pendulumlike arcs above the female; at the top of each swoop he comes to a dead stop and taps his wings together underneath his body.

Woodpeckers *Picitae*

Specially suited for scaling trees, woodpeckers have stiff tail feathers for prop-
ping themselves against trunks. Their feet (except for those of the Three-toed
Woodpecker and the Black-backed Woodpecker) are each equipped with
four strong toes, two facing forward and two, backward. Woodpeckers use
their straight, pointed bills for chiseling wood in search of sap and insects and
for excavating cavities for nesting and roosting. Some species, such as hairy
woodpeckers and sapsuckers, prefer to work on live trees; others, such as
flickers and downies, choose dying or dead trees.

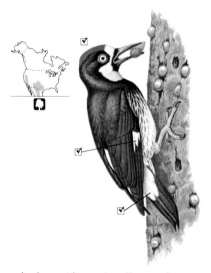

Acorn Woodpecker
Melanerpes formicivorus

LENGTH:
8½-9½ in.

WHAT TO LOOK FOR:
red, black, and white pattern on head
and neck; upper parts mostly black,
with white wing patch and rump.

HABITAT:
stands of oak, mixed woodlands,
canyons, foothills with scattered trees.

The Acorn-storing Woodpecker, as it used
to be called, drills small holes in trees and
packs them with nuts (usually acorns), one to each hole. One packed ponderosa pine was
studded with an estimated 50,000 acorns. The Acorn Woodpecker is remarkable, too, for its
breeding habits. Unlike other woodpeckers, it is very social and often nests in colonies of a
dozen or so. Several pairs may even share in digging a nest hole and then cooperate in incubating the eggs and raising the young.

Pileated Woodpecker

Dryocopus pileatus

LENGTH:
14-18½ in.

WHAT TO LOOK FOR:
large size; red crest; black, white, and
red pattern on head; mostly black, with
white wing linings conspicuous in
flight.

HABITAT:
mature forests.

The slow, rhythmic hammering of a
Pileated Woodpecker may be mistaken for
the sound of a man chopping down a tree.
With powerful whacks the bird digs a
large rectangular or oval hole deep into
the heart of a tree infested with carpenter
ants, a principal food. Fresh chips at the
base of a tree indicate a hole that is still
being dug.

MALE

FEMALE

Red-bellied Woodpecker

Melanerpes carolinus

LENGTH:
8-10 in.

WHAT TO LOOK FOR:
fine black and white barring on back; red nape; red crown (male); white patch near end of wings visible in flight.

HABITAT:
forest, groves, orchards, farmland, suburbs.

This abundant southern species is now expanding its range to the north. In the South the Red-belly occasionally feeds on oranges, but it makes up for this by eating quantities of destructive insects. It most often nests in a dead tree at the edge of a woodland, frequently using the same hole year after year. The female lays unspotted white eggs, usually four or five in a clutch. (This is typical of woodpeckers.) The name Red-bellied Woodpecker is misleading, for the red patch on its belly is rather faint.

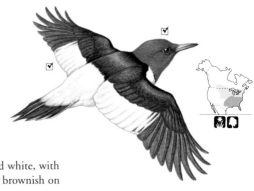

Red-headed Woodpecker

Melanerpes erythrocephalus

LENGTH:
7-10 in.

WHAT TO LOOK FOR:
red head and neck; mostly black and white, with large white wing patches; immature brownish on head and back.

HABITAT:
open woods, groves, swamps with dead trees.

Northern Flicker
Colaptes auratus

LENGTH:
10-13 in.

WHAT TO LOOK FOR:
white rump; black crescent at throat; yellow or red on underside of wings and tail (in East, yellow only); male with "mustache" of black (East) or red (West).

HABITAT:
deserts, farmlands, suburbs, parks, open forests.

This unusual woodpecker is often seen on the ground, searching for ants and licking them up with its long tongue. It does, however, nest in holes in trees—or tree substitutes such as telephone poles. Flickers are conspicuous in fall, when they often travel in loose flocks. In spring their arrival is announced by noisy calls— *wick-a, wick-a, wick-a.*

◀ **Red-headed Woodpecker** (AT LEFT) The diet of the Red-headed Woodpecker is notably varied. It includes beechnuts, acorns, corn, fruits, insects, and the eggs and young of small birds. Like several other woodpeckers, this species has the habit of storing food for future use. Grasshoppers are stuffed into crevices in fence posts, and nuts are packed into knotholes and into cracks in buildings. Wherever nut trees are abundant and productive, there is a good chance of seeing this woodpecker and hearing its loud *quee-o, quee-o, queer.*

Three-toed Woodpecker
Picoides tridactylus

LENGTH:
7-9 in.

WHAT TO LOOK FOR:
yellow crown (male); back with black and white bars or jagged white patch; barred sides; wings mostly black.

HABITAT:
coniferous forests.

The Three-toed Woodpecker is an unusual bird. It is the only woodpecker that lives both in North America and Eurasia. It has two toes pointing forward, one pointing backward. Except for the similar Black-backed Woodpecker (*Picoides arcticus*), other woodpeckers have four toes. Males of both species have yellow head patches, not red. And instead of hammering into trees, as most woodpeckers do, they flake off sheets of bark from dead trees and feed on the wood borers and beetles underneath.

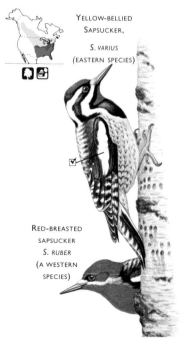

YELLOW-BELLIED SAPSUCKER,

S. VARIUS
(EASTERN SPECIES)

Yellow-bellied Sapsucker
Sphyrapicus varius

LENGTH:
7-8½ in.

WHAT TO LOOK FOR:
long white wing stripe; black, white, and red pattern on head and neck; immature brownish, with wing stripe.

HABITAT:
forests, woodlands, orchards; parks (migration).

RED-BREASTED SAPSUCKER
S. RUBER
(A WESTERN SPECIES)

Downy Woodpecker

Picoides pubescens

LENGTH:
5-6½ in.

WHAT TO LOOK FOR:
small size; short bill; black and white pattern on head and wings; white back; red patch on head (male).

HABITAT:
woodlands, orchards, suburbs, parks.

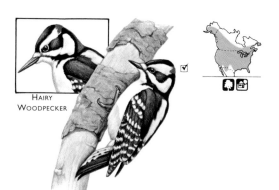

HAIRY
WOODPECKER

The little Downy is probably our most familiar woodpecker. In winter it readily takes suet from bird feeders and often joins the mixed bands of small birds that roam through the woods, each species feeding in a different manner but all deriving protection from the wariness of the flock. The larger Hairy Woodpecker (*Picoides villosus*) is more of a forest dweller than the Downy. Both "Downies" and "Hairies" are named for their feathers, probably the short ones around their nostrils.

◀ **Yellow-bellied Sapsucker** (AT LEFT) Unlike other woodpeckers, sapsuckers have brushlike tongues, not barbed ones, and cannot extract wood-boring insects from a tree. Instead, they drill neat rows of holes (primarily in birches and orchard trees), remove the nutritious inner bark, and later eat the sap that has run out, as well as the insects trapped in it. There are four species in North America.

attacking a crow

Eastern Kingbird
Tyrannus tyrannus

LENGTH:
7-9 in.

WHAT TO LOOK FOR:
blackish above, white below; dark tail with
prominent white band at tip; flies with
stiff, shallow wingbeats from a high perch.

HABITAT:
forest edges; woodlands and open areas
with occasional tall trees.

Thoreau called this flycatcher a "lively bird," and wrote that its noisy twittering "stirs and
keeps the air brisk." The Eastern Kingbird is not only lively; it is fearless in defense of its
territory. It will attack any passing crow or hawk, flying at it from above, pecking at the
victim and pulling out feathers; it may even land on the flying intruder. The Gray
Kingbird (*Tyrannus dominicensis*) is a slightly larger and paler bird of Florida and nearby
coastal areas. Its bill is large, and it has no band on its notched tail.

Western Kingbird

Tyrannus verticalis

LENGTH:
7-9 in.

WHAT TO LOOK FOR:
outer tail feathers white; cap, nape, and
back gray; throat white; underparts yellow.

HABITAT:
arid open areas with scattered trees or tall
brush; wooded stream valleys; farmlands.

This species, like other flycatchers, hunts from a perch. It flies out, plucks an insect from
the air, and then sails back, often to the same spot. Adults teach their young to hunt by
catching insects, disabling them, and releasing them for the young to fetch. A similar
western species is Cassin's Kingbird (*Tyrannus vociferans*), with a darker breast and no
white outer tail feathers.

Flycatchers *Empidonax*

Flycatcher identification: some clues. The 10 small *Empidonax* flycatchers—3 of which are shown below—are among the most difficult of our birds to identify. They are all 4 to 6 inches long; most have a dark back, a pale front, a pale eye ring, and two pale wingbars. Slight differences in color can help distinguish some species, and habitat is sometimes a useful clue. But in most cases the only way to tell one *Empidonax* flycatcher from another is by voice; their calls are usually distinctive. However, all of these flycatchers tend to be silent except during the breeding season. At other times of the year most people just give up precise identification and write "*Empidonax*, species?" in their field notebooks.

Great Crested Flycatcher

Myiarchus crinitus

LENGTH:
7-9 in.

WHAT TO LOOK FOR:
reddish-brown tail and wing patch; yellow belly; whitish wingbars; slight crest.

HABITAT:
forests, clusters of trees.

This handsome bird announces its presence with a loud, clear *wheep* or rolling *crrreep*. The Great Crested Flycatcher always nests in a cavity—an abandoned woodpecker hole, a hollow tree, or a nest box. If the hole is too deep, the birds will fill it up from the bottom with debris before beginning the nest of twigs. They may add a cast-off snakeskin or a strip of shiny plastic, which is sometimes left hanging outside the cavity. In dry parts of the West the smaller Ash-throated Flycatcher (*Myiarchus cinerascens*) often nests in a hole in a large cactus.

Scissor-tailed Flycatcher

Tyrannus forficatus

LENGTH:
11-15½ in.

WHAT TO LOOK FOR:
tail deeply forked, with extremely long
feathers; pale gray above, with small rose
shoulder patch; whitish below, shading to
pink on flanks, belly, and underwings;
immature less pink with shorter tail.

HABITAT:
open brushy areas with scattered trees,
poles, wires, or other high perches.

The male Scissor-tailed Flycatcher shows off in a remarkable courtship flight. Flying up
to perhaps 100 feet above the ground, he begins a series of short, abrupt dives and
climbs, ending the sequence by falling into two or three consecutive somersaults. Scissor-
tails hunt insects from elevated perches and on the ground, seemingly unencumbered by
their long tails. Adults of both sexes have the long, streaming plumes.

Black Phoebe

Sayornis nigricans

LENGTH:
5½-7 in.

WHAT TO LOOK FOR:
only flycatcher with black throat and breast; belly and outer tailfeathers white; sits erect and wags tail.

HABITAT:
shaded streams and ponds, wooded or brushy areas, farmlands, suburbs.

The Black Phoebe breeds near water, often locating its nest on a bridge girder or even down a well; buildings, trees, and cliffs are other nesting sites. A shaded low branch overhanging a pool or stream is a favorite perch. The Black Phoebe's call—*tsip* or *chee*—is repeated frequently, accompanied by flicks of its tail. The song is a plaintive *ti-wee, ti-wee*. Of the three phoebes, this is the only species that usually does not migrate.

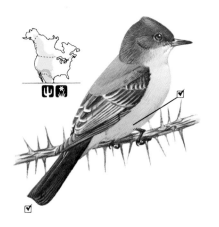

Say's Phoebe

Sayornis saya

LENGTH:
6-7½ in.

WHAT TO LOOK FOR:
lower breast and belly rusty; upperparts grayish; tail blackish; wags tail.

HABITAT:
open desert, semiarid areas, ranchlands, brushy fields, canyon mouths.

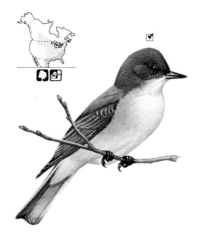

Eastern Phoebe

Sayornis phoebe

LENGTH:
5-7 in.

WHAT TO LOOK FOR:
brownish olive above, with darker head; whitish below, with gray breast; sits upright on perch and wags tail frequently.

HABITAT:
woodlands, farmlands, suburbs; usually near water.

Fibrit, says the Eastern Phoebe emphatically from its perch, wagging its tail in characteristic motion. Phoebes are not shy. Often they are found in or on porches, garages, barns, and bridges, nesting on a ledge or beam. This species made ornithological history in 1803 when Audubon tied silver thread on the legs of nestlings—the first North American experiment in bird banding. The next year he found that two of his marked birds had returned and were nesting nearby.

◀ **Say's Phoebe** (AT LEFT) This dry country flycatcher replaces the Eastern Phoebe in much of the West and has similar habits. It is a tail wagger, and it often nests on or around ranch buildings. Its call, however, is different— a low, plaintive *phee-eur.* Its customary perch is on top of a small bush, a tall weed stalk, or a low rock. In the northern portion of its range, Say's Phoebe is migratory, but it is a year-round resident in warmer areas.

Yellow-bellied Flycatcher

Empidonax flaviventris

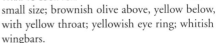

LENGTH:
4½-5½ in.

WHAT TO LOOK FOR:
small size; brownish olive above, yellow below, with yellow throat; yellowish eye ring; whitish wingbars.

HABITAT:
northern coniferous forests, bogs, alder thickets, mixed woodlands (migration).

A bird of the wet northern forests, the Yellow-bellied Flycatcher nests on the ground or not far above it, in the side of a moss-covered bank or in the fern-draped earth clinging to the roots of a fallen tree. Its song is an upward-sliding *chee-weep*, sweet and melancholy; it also utters a short *killick*. In breeding plumage this species shows more yellow than any of its relatives in its range—the Least (below), the Willow (*Empidonax traillii*), or the Alder (*Empidonax alnorum*). The Acadian Flycatcher (*Empidonax virescens*) is a southeastern species, but it too is a bird of wet woods and streamsides, and on migration may be found in the same places as the Yellow-bellied.

Least Flycatcher

Empidonax minimus

LENGTH:
4½-5 in.

WHAT TO LOOK FOR:
small size; belly white or pale yellow; head and back olive-gray; whitish eye ring and wingbars.

HABITAT:
open forests, orchards, rural towns, suburbs, parks.

Western Flycatcher

Empidonax difficilis
Empidonax occidentalis

LENGTH:
5-6 in.

WHAT TO LOOK FOR:
yellow throat and belly; olive-brown back;
whitish eye ring and wingbars.

HABITAT:
moist coniferous and mixed forests,
deciduous groves, wooded canyons.

Scientists have decided that the Western
Flycatcher is actually two species separated by geography, the Pacific-slope
(*Empidonax difficilis*) of the coast and the Cordilleran (*Empidonax occidentalis*) of
the Rockies. The green moss nest of the Western Flycatcher, lined with shredded
bark, is always located in damp woods—often near a stream and sometimes even
under the lip of a streambank. (It may also build as high as 30 feet up in a tree.)
Two close relatives of the Western Flycatcher, which also occur within its range,
are best identified by habitat. Hammond's Flycatcher (*Empidonax hammondii*)
breeds in high coniferous forests. The Dusky Flycatcher (*Empidonax oberholseri*) is
a bird of the foothill chaparral and of brushy mountain slopes. Both species have
similar calls and look very much alike.

◀ **Least Flycatcher** (AT LEFT) The Least Flycatcher is noisy during the
breeding season. Its curt *chebec* is given as often as 75 times a
minute, and it may go on repeating itself for several hours at a time.
The male sometimes adds a warble—*chebec-trree-treo, chebec-treee-
chou.* Other notes include one-syllable *whit* calls. The species nests in
both conifers and deciduous trees, usually quite low but at times as
high as 60 feet. The deep little cup is frequently nestled in the crotch
of a limb; materials include shreds of bark, plant down, spiderweb,
fine woody stems, and grasses. Southerly nesters may raise two
broods a year.

Olive-sided Flycatcher

Contopus borealis

LENGTH:
6-7½ in.

WHAT TO LOOK FOR:
grayish brown above, white below, with brown-streaked sides; white patch below wing sometimes visible.

HABITAT:
coniferous and mixed woodlands, forest-edged bogs, swamps with dead trees; eucalyptus groves (California).

Perched on top of a tall tree or dead snag, the Olive-sided Flycatcher whistles a cheery *pip-whee-beer*. The first note, *pip*, is inaudible at a distance, but the rest of the song is high and clear. When alarmed, this husky flycatcher calls *pip-pip-pip*. The Greater Pewee (*Contopus pertinax*) of the southwestern mountains resembles the Olive-sided, but lacks the streaked sides and white patches.

Vermilion Flycatcher

Pyrocephalus rubinus

LENGTH:
5-6 in.

WHAT TO LOOK FOR:
male with brilliant red cap and underparts, dark brown back, wings, and tail; female brown above, light below, with fine streaking and pink wash on sides.

HABITAT:
wooded streamsides in arid regions; groves near water.

FEMALE

MALE

Eastern Wood-pewee

Contopus virens

LENGTH:
5-6 in.

WHAT TO LOOK FOR:
brownish olive above, whitish below; conspicuous white wing-bars; no eye ring.

HABITAT:
mature deciduous forests, other woodlands, especially along rivers.

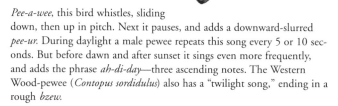

Pee-a-wee, this bird whistles, sliding down, then up in pitch. Next it pauses, and adds a downward-slurred *pee-ur.* During daylight a male pewee repeats this song every 5 or 10 seconds. But before dawn and after sunset it sings even more frequently, and adds the phrase *ah-di-day*—three ascending notes. The Western Wood-pewee (*Contopus sordidulus*) also has a "twilight song," ending in a rough *bzew.*

◄ **Vermilion Flycatcher** (AT LEFT) The courting male is very conspicuous as he circles up on rapidly beating wings, pausing often to give his tinkling song. He may climb as high as 50 feet before swooping down to perch near his mate. The nest, usually built into a horizontal crotch of a willow or mesquite, is a flat saucer of twigs, weeds, hair, and feathers, tied down with spider silk.

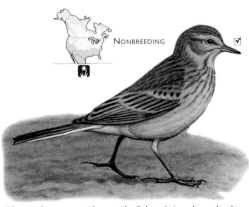

American Pipit

Anthus rubescens

LENGTH: 5-6½ in.

WHAT TO LOOK FOR:

slim shape; thin bill; dark above, streaked below (breeding bird paler, less streaked); white outer tail feathers; frequently wags tail.

HABITAT:

tundra, alpine meadows; grasslands, beaches, coasts (migration).

This is the more widespread of the pipits; the paler-legged Sprague's Pipit (*Anthus spragueii*) occurs in a swath down the center of the continent. Both species walk, instead of hopping like the sparrows they resemble. (Pipits and sparrows actually belong to two very different families.) In courtship, singing males fly almost straight up as high as 200 feet, then float down on fluttering wings.

Horned Lark

Eremophila alpestris

LENGTH:
6-7½ in.

WHAT TO LOOK FOR:
chest and head patterned with black and yellow; black tail with white on outside; "horns" not always visible.

HABITAT:
stony deserts, tundra, grasslands, other open spaces, shore areas.

The Horned Lark is a bird of the bare earth, where it nests and feeds, and the sky, where it soars, sings, and plummets downward once again. In the fall individuals from the Far North migrate in large flocks, joining the local breeding birds wherever they find their preferred habitat—ground with a minimum of low vegetation to supply the seeds on which they feed. This is North America's only true lark.

Gray Jay

Perisoreus canadensis

LENGTH:
9½-12½ in.

WHAT TO LOOK FOR:
gray with dark nape, white throat, and white forehead; immature gray, with light "mustache."

HABITAT:
coniferous forests, upland aspen and birch groves.

ADULT

IMMATURE

This is the Wis-ka-tjon of the Indians, the Whiskey Jack or Camp Robber of the white trappers, and the Canada Jay of old-time ornithology. A boldly confident bird, it hangs around forest camps, exploring even inside the tents and stealing food, soap, candles, and tobacco. Gray Jays nest while snow still covers the ground, and often line the nest with feathers for warmth. They seldom migrate except in "famine" years, when flocks of them drift south.

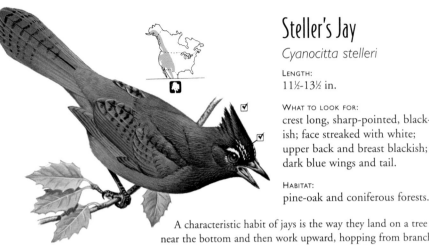

Steller's Jay

Cyanocitta stelleri

LENGTH:
11½-13½ in.

WHAT TO LOOK FOR:
crest long, sharp-pointed, blackish; face streaked with white; upper back and breast blackish; dark blue wings and tail.

HABITAT:
pine-oak and coniferous forests.

A characteristic habit of jays is the way they land on a tree near the bottom and then work upward, hopping from branch to branch until they reach the top. Then they leave, perhaps to repeat the maneuver. Steller's Jays, like their relatives, build bulky nests of dead leaves and twigs, usually near the trunk of a conifer.

Blue Jay

Cyanocitta cristata

LENGTH:
9½-12 in.

WHAT TO LOOK FOR:
pointed crest; black "necklace;" bright blue above, with white on wings and tail.

HABITAT:
woodlands, farmlands, suburbs, city parks.

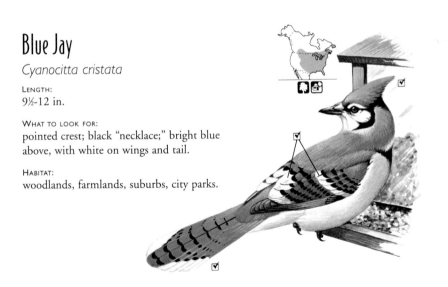

Scrub Jay

Aphelocoma coerulescens

LENGTH:
9½-12 in.

WHAT TO LOOK FOR:
no crest; head, wings, and tail blue; mostly white below.

HABITAT:
scrub oak chaparral; pinyon-juniper woodlands; palmetto-pine thickets (Florida).

The Scrub Jays have separated into several forms in Florida and the West, as have the Burrowing Owl, the Sandhill Crane, and certain other species. The wide gap in distribution may have been caused by changes in climate, habitat, or food supply. The Scrub Jays have become different enough to be considered three species: the Florida Scrub Jay (*Aphelocoma coerulescens*), the Western Scrub Jay (*Aphelocoma californica*), and the Island Scrub Jay (*Aphelocoma insularis*). The Mexican Jay (*Aphelocoma ultramarina*) of the mountains of the Southwest is duller and lacks the blue necklace of the Scrub Jays.

◀ **Blue Jay** (AT LEFT) This handsome, noisy bird is known for its raucous voice and the wide variety of its calls, cries, and screams. But like other jays, it also has a "whisper song," a series of faint whistles and soft, sweet notes delivered from a perch hidden in foliage. Blue Jays are omnivorous, feeding on (among other things) fruits, seeds, nuts, insects, birds' eggs, small birds, mice, treefrogs, snails, and even fish. In spring and fall these jays migrate in flocks that sometimes number in the hundreds.

YELLOW-
BILLED
MAGPIE

Black-billed Magpie

Pica pica

LENGTH:
17½-21½ in.

WHAT TO LOOK FOR:
tail long, tapering, metallic green; bold black and white pattern in flight.

HABITAT:
open forests; brushy areas of prairies and foothills; bottomland groves; ranches.

This conspicuous, long-tailed species constructs a particularly strong nest in a bush or low in a tree. Sticks, often thorny, make up the base and walls. Mud or fresh dung mixed with vegetation is packed inside, and the cup is lined with roots, stems, and hair. Over the nest the birds build a dome of sticks—again, often thorny. The Yellow-billed Magpie (*Pica nuttalli*) of California builds the same sort of nest.

Clark's Nutcracker

Nucifraga columbiana

LENGTH:
12-13 in.

WHAT TO LOOK FOR:
body light gray; wings and tail black, with white patches; bill long, pointed.

HABITAT:
coniferous forests near tree line; lower slopes, isolated groves.

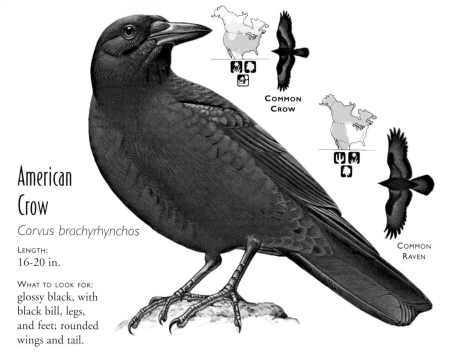

COMMON CROW

COMMON RAVEN

American Crow

Corvus brachyrhynchos

LENGTH:
16-20 in.

WHAT TO LOOK FOR:
glossy black, with black bill, legs, and feet; rounded wings and tail.

HABITAT:
forests; woods near water; open areas; farmlands; suburbs.

Judged by human standards, crows are perhaps the most intelligent of birds. They can count at least to three or four; they quickly learn new information; they appear to have a complex language and well-developed social structure. North America has three kinds, the American Crow and two smaller species usually found near the shore—the Northwestern and the Fish Crow (*Corvus caurinus* and *ossifragus*). A Mexican species also visits Texas. The Common and the Chihuahuan Raven (*Corvus corax* and *cryptoleucus*), larger birds with wedge-shaped tails, are sometimes mistaken for crows.

◀ Clark's Nutcracker (AT LEFT) William Clark, of the Lewis and Clark expedition, thought this bird was a woodpecker, but the leading American ornithologist of the day, Alexander Wilson, called it a crow. Clark's Nutcracker has the woodpecker's bounding flight at times; at other times it flies more directly, like a crow. It pecks at cones and nuts like a woodpecker, and robs the nests of other birds, as crows do.

Tree Swallow

Tachycineta bicolor

LENGTH:
4½-5½ in.

WHAT TO LOOK FOR:
glossy blue-black or greenish above (immature dark brown), white below; tail slightly forked.

HABITAT:
open areas with scattered trees and dead stubs; usually near water.

This is the hardiest swallow, arriving early in spring and even wintering over in some localities. When insects are unavailable, Tree Swallows feed mostly on bayberries; some wintering birds have also been seen picking seeds from pond ice. Tree Swallows will nest in birdhouses and mailboxes, as well as in holes in dead tree stubs, their natural nesting sites. In fall the brown-backed immatures can be mistaken for Bank Swallows (*Riparia riparia*), which have brown "collars," and for Rough-winged Swallows (*Stelgidopteryx serripennis*), which have a brown wash on the throat. In the West, adult birds can be confused with Violet-green Swallows (*Tachycineta thalassina*), a species with more white on the lower back.

Cliff Swallow

Hirundo pyrrhonota

LENGTH: 5-6 in.

WHAT TO LOOK FOR: mostly dark above; light forehead; rusty rump and throat; square tail.

HABITAT: open country cliffs, farmlands with bridges or buildings for nesting; usually near water.

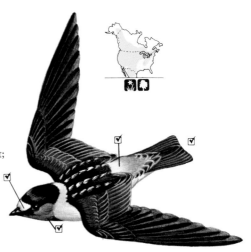

Barn Swallow

Hirundo rustica

LENGTH:
5½-7 in.

WHAT TO LOOK FOR:
tail deeply forked; glossy
dark blue above;
light rufous below,
with darker throat.

HABITAT:
open woodlands, other open areas,
farmlands, suburbs.

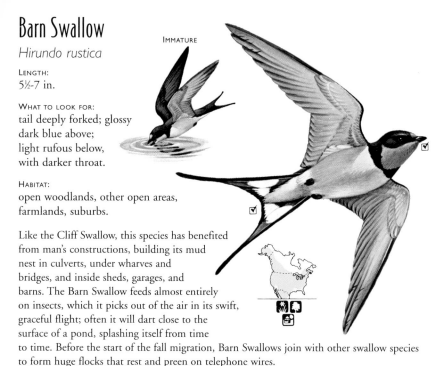

IMMATURE

Like the Cliff Swallow, this species has benefited
from man's constructions, building its mud
nest in culverts, under wharves and
bridges, and inside sheds, garages, and
barns. The Barn Swallow feeds almost entirely
on insects, which it picks out of the air in its swift,
graceful flight; often it will dart close to the
surface of a pond, splashing itself from time
to time. Before the start of the fall migration, Barn Swallows join with other swallow species
to form huge flocks that rest and preen on telephone wires.

◀ **Cliff Swallow** (AT LEFT) After it was reported from Hudson Bay in 1772, no naturalist
noticed the Cliff Swallow—or mentioned it, anyway—until 1815, when Audubon found a
few in Kentucky. From then on, the birds were seen in many parts of North America.
Probably they had simply been overlooked all those years. Quite likely, Cliff Swallows
began appearing where people could get a look at them as they gradually discovered the
suitability of nest sites under the eaves of houses and barns (cliffsides are their natural nest
sites). These are the swallows that return to the Mission of San Juan Capistrano, in
California, on or about March 19 each year.

Purple Martin

Progne subis

MALE

FEMALE

LENGTH:
7-8 in.

WHAT TO LOOK FOR:
largest swallow; tail slightly forked; male glossy blue-black; female duller above, with mottled throat and whitish belly.

HABITAT:
open areas, scattered woodlands, farmlands, suburbs; usually near water.

Purple Martins have a long history of nesting in shelters supplied by man. In the past they used hollow gourds hung by Indians, and today the species is largely dependent on martin houses. These birds have a strong homing instinct, demonstrated by a colony that returned one spring to find its apartment house gone. The martins hovered and circled at the precise spot in midair where the house had been.

Black-capped Chickadee

Parus atricapillus

LENGTH:
4½-5½ in.

WHAT TO LOOK FOR:
mostly light gray; black cap and throat; white cheek patch.

HABITAT:
mixed and deciduous forests, suburbs, parks.

Chickadees that look somewhat alike can often be told apart by their sounds. *Fee-bee*, the Black-capped Chickadee whistles, the first note of the song a full tone higher than the second. Its call is the familiar *chick-a-dee*. In the Middle West and Southeast the Carolina Chickadee (*Parus carolinensis*) whistles a longer, more sibilant *su-fee, su-bee*, ending on a low note. Its *chick-a-dee* calls are more rapid.

Boreal Chickadee

Parus hudsonicus

LENGTH:
4½-5 in.

WHAT TO LOOK FOR:
brown cap and back; red-brown sides; black throat.

HABITAT:
northern coniferous forests.

The Boreal Chickadee seldom wanders far from its northern breeding range. But some winters the "brown caps" move southward in great numbers, probably inspired by a dwindling supply of insect eggs, larvae, and conifer seeds. Boreal Chickadees sing their *chick-a-dee* in a drawling, buzzy voice. The Chestnut-backed Chickadee (*Parus rufescens*), found along the Pacific coast and inland to Idaho and Montana, has a shriller, more explosive call.

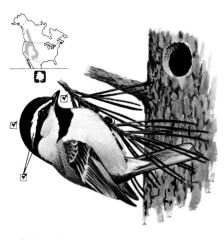

Mountain Chickadee

Parus gambeli

LENGTH:
4½-5½ in.

WHAT TO LOOK FOR:
black line through white cheek patch; black cap and throat.

HABITAT:
oak-pine and coniferous mountain forests; mixed forests at lower elevations (winter).

All the chickadees nest in cavities, usually in living trees but occasionally in nest boxes and even in holes in the ground. Some species, like the Black-capped Chickadee, chop out their own holes in rotting wood. The Mountain Chickadee uses natural cavities or old woodpecker holes that need little enlarging. After the young are raised, this high-altitude species, like the other chickadees, joins mixed flocks of small birds that circulate through the forest as they feed.

Tufted Titmouse

Parus bicolor

LENGTH:
5½-6 in.

WHAT TO LOOK FOR:
gray with buffy flanks; gray crest (black in Texas).

HABITAT:
deciduous forests, cypress swamps, pine woods, wooded bottomlands, orchards, suburbs.

Long regarded as a southern species, the Tufted Titmouse has been spreading northward in recent years. Now these tame, confiding birds are familiar visitors at feeders from Michigan to New England. Their ringing song varies; usually it is a rapid two-note whistle—*pe-ter, pe-ter*. Titmice are relatives of the chickadees, and this species has a number of chickadeelike calls. In the West, the Plain Titmouse (*Parus inornatus*), which lacks the buffy flanks of the Tufted, actually does call *tsick-a-dee-dee*.

Verdin

Auriparus flaviceps

LENGTH:
4-4½ in.

WHAT TO LOOK FOR:
small size; grayish, with yellow on head (paler on female) and chestnut shoulder patch.

HABITAT:
semiarid or arid regions with scattered thorny scrub and mesquite.

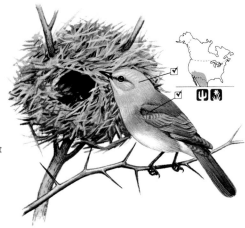

Wrentit

Chamaea fasciata

LENGTH
5-6 in.

WHAT TO LOOK FOR:
brown bird with streaked breast; tail long, rounded, often erect; light eye.

HABITAT:
chaparral, brushy areas, suburbs, parks.

Once it is located by its loud, whistling song, this little bird is difficult to watch. It seldom flies any distance or perches in the open, but instead moves about stealthily in dense brush. Much of what is known about the Wrentit is due to an observer who studied a population in a California canyon. Among other discoveries, she found that at night roosting pairs sit side by side and shuffle their body feathers so that they become enveloped in a single bundle of plumage.

◄ **Verdin** (AT LEFT) A remarkable nest builder, the Verdin weaves a round, long-lasting shell of stout, thorny twigs. The nest is lined with plant down and other plant material, spider silk, and feathers. Inside the entrance is a high "doorstep" that discourages intruders. The Verdin usually locates its nest conspicuously in a cactus, thorny bush, or small tree, choosing a fork at the end of a low branch. These structures are also used for roosting and winter shelter.

White-breasted Nuthatch

Sitta carolinensis

LENGTH:
5-6 in.

WHAT TO LOOK FOR:
black crown and nape; blue-gray above, white below; bill long, straight.

HABITAT:
mixed and deciduous forests, woods; groves; suburbs.

The nuthatches are the only birds that habitually climb down tree trunks headfirst, gathering insects and insect eggs from crevices and under the bark. The name nuthatch derives from *nut-hack*, for the way the birds wedge nuts and other food into crevices and chop them into pieces. The southeastern Brown-headed Nuthatch (*Sitta pusilla*) and the western Pygmy Nuthatch (*Sitta pygmaea*) are smaller species.

Red-breasted Nuthatch

Sitta canadensis

LENGTH:
3½-4½ in.

WHAT TO LOOK FOR:
white line above eye; black cap; blue-gray back; reddish underparts.

HABITAT:
coniferous forests; mixed woodlands (mainly in winter).

The Red-breasted Nuthatch usually digs its nest hole in dead wood, but it may also use natural cavities, old woodpecker holes, and nest boxes. Whatever site it chooses, it always smears the entrance hole with pitch from spruce, fir, or pine, perhaps to discourage predators. This nuthatch is an active little bird, scurrying over tree trunks and branches, dashing from tree to tree, and calling *yna, yna, yna, yna* in a thin, nasal voice. The White-breasted species has a lower-pitched call.

Brown Creeper

Certhia americana

LENGTH:
4½-5½ in.

WHAT TO LOOK FOR:
streaked brown above, white below; bill long, slender, curved down.

HABITAT:
mixed and coniferous forests, groves, woods.

The spring song of the Brown Creeper is a high, sweet phrase, surprisingly different from its usual thin *sssst*. But since the spring song is ventriloquistic, the bird can be difficult to locate. In feeding the Brown Creeper invariably flies to the bottom of a tree and gradually hitches its way up the trunk in its search for insects. Then it drops to the bottom of another tree and begins hitching upward once again.

White-breasted
Nuthatch

Red-breasted
Nuthatch

Brown Creeper

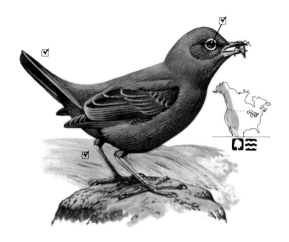

American Dipper

Cinclus mexicanus

LENGTH:
5½-8 in.

WHAT TO LOOK FOR:
stocky bird; slate-gray, with white eye ring; legs long, yellowish; short tail; bobs continually.

HABITAT:
fast-flowing mountain streams.

Dippers are so dependent on water that they are seldom seen flying even short distances over dry land. A dipper collects its food—aquatic insects and small fry—by diving into the water and wading submerged along the bottom. In Alaska dippers have been seen flitting around the icy edges of open water holes and diving when the air temperature was far below zero. The nest is built under a streambank or waterfall.

Bushtit

Psaltriparus minimus

LENGTH:
3-4 in.

WHAT TO LOOK FOR:
small grayish bird with long tail;
brown cap (Rocky Mountain race
with gray cap and brown cheeks);
male in extreme Southwest with
black mask.

HABITAT:
mixed woodlands; stands of scrub
oak, pinyon, or juniper; chaparral.

Bushtits are small, inconspicuous birds that build
elaborate nests. A pair begins by constructing a more
or less horizontal rim between adjacent twigs. With
this as a frame, the birds weave a small sack and gradually stretch and strengthen it, working mostly from
inside. A hood and an entrance hole are added at the
top. Materials vary with the locality, but usually the
nest is held together with spiderweb and decorated
with bits of moss and lichen.

House Wren

Troglodytes aedon

LENGTH:
4-5 in.

WHAT TO LOOK FOR:
gray-brown above, lighter below, with barring on wings and tail; tail often held erect.

HABITAT:
open woodlands, forest edges, shrubby areas, suburbs, parks.

House Wrens are aggressive and adaptable nesters. They will build their nests in just about any container left out in the open—flowerpot, empty tin can, pocket of an old coat—as well as tree holes and nest boxes. They often bully other birds, ejecting them from nest sites and even destroying eggs and young. Two broods a season are raised. The male frequently changes partners in mid-season, so that while his original mate is still feeding chicks, another female is sitting on new eggs.

Carolina Wren

Thryothorus ludovicianus

LENGTH:
4½-5½ in.

WHAT TO LOOK FOR:
wide white eye stripe; rufous above,
with white throat and tawny sides.

HABITAT:
forests with dense undergrowth;
scrubby areas; thickets; brush near water.

The loud, ringing call of the Carolina Wren is one of the commonest sounds
of southeastern woods, where it is heard even in winter. The call is usually a
series of double or triple notes, written as *cheery, cheery, cheery* or *tea-kettle,
tea-kettle, tea-kettle*. The bird has been called "mocking wren" because it
sometimes sounds like a catbird, a kingfisher, or certain other kinds of birds.

Marsh Wren

Cistothorus palustris

LENGTH:
4-5 in.

WHAT TO LOOK FOR:
brown cap; wide white eye stripe; streaked upper back; reddish lower back; white underparts.

HABITAT:
freshwater and brackish marshes.

Because of both habits and habitats, some wrens are heard more often than seen. The furtive Marsh Wren may pop out only briefly from thick stands of reeds, cattails, and marsh grasses to give its sputtering song. The Sedge Wren (*Cistothorus platensis*), of sedgy bogs and wet meadows in the East, is very secretive. It sings a thin, dry *tip, tip, tip-trrrrrrr.*

Winter Wren

Troglodytes troglodytes

LENGTH:
3-4 in.

WHAT TO LOOK FOR:
small size; reddish brown, with dark
barring on flanks; very short tail.

HABITAT:
coniferous and mixed forests with
heavy undergrowth, often near
streams; wooded swamps.

The song of the Winter Wren is clear, rapid, and very high in pitch,
often with notes beyond the range of human ears. The wren sings
along at 16 notes a second, stringing beautiful, tinkling passages
into long pieces. It sings over the sound of surf on remote Alaskan
islands, where it nests on cliffs and rocky slopes near the shore.
Elsewhere it is most often a bird of the deep woods, nesting in the
earth that clings to the roots of fallen trees, under standing roots,
or in crevices between rocks.

Bewick's Wren

Thryomanes bewickii

LENGTH:
4½-5½ in.

WHAT TO LOOK FOR:
white eye stripe; brown above, white below; tail long, with white spots on outer feathers.

HABITAT:
woodlands, brushy areas, chaparral, suburbs.

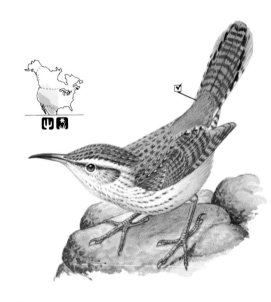

Audubon named this species for a British friend, Thomas Bewick (pronounced "buick"), whose wood engravings of birds were famous in his day. Though somewhat larger than the House Wren, Bewick's Wren is less aggressive, and it usually loses out when the two species compete for space. Its diet, like that of all wrens, consists almost entirely of insects, spiders, and other small invertebrates; Bewick's Wren in particular is credited with destroying many injurious species such as scale insects and bark beetles.

Rock Wren

Salpinctes obsoletus

LENGTH:
4½-6 in.

WHAT TO LOOK FOR:
upper parts grayish brown, with rufous rump; throat and breast white, finely streaked with brown.

HABITAT:
deserts; high, dry meadows; rocky areas.

Cactus Wren

Campylorhynchus brunneicapillus

LENGTH:
6-8½ in.

WHAT TO LOOK FOR:
large size; white eye stripe;
throat and breast heavily spotted
with black; wings and tail
barred with black.

HABITAT:
brushy desert areas with cactus, yucca,
and mesquite.

The largest wren is a bird of arid, low-altitude country where cacti are plentiful. Its nest is conspicuous—a domed affair with a tunnel entrance 5 or 6 inches long. The whole structure, woven of plant fibers, leaves, and twigs, is shaped rather like a flask lying on its side. Typically, it is placed in the arms of a big cactus or on a branch of a thorny bush or mesquite tree. A pair of Cactus Wrens will maintain several nests at one time and may raise three broods a year, changing nests at the beginning of each cycle. After the young have left, the adults continue to make repairs, since the nests are used as winter roosts.

◀ **Rock Wren** (AT LEFT) The Rock Wren is a loud, rough-voiced, and garrulous singer with the habit of repeating itself. One listener wrote: "*Keree keree, keree, keree,* he says. *Chair, chair, chair, chair, deedle, deedle, deedle, deedle, tur, tur, tur, tur, keree, keree, keree, trrrrrrrrr.*" The Rock Wren nests in holes in the earth, between boulders, or under loose stones, often on slopes. It usually paves the floor beneath and around its nest with small stones and sometimes also with bones and assorted trash. Another western species of about the same size is the white-breasted Canyon Wren (*Catherpes mexicanus*).

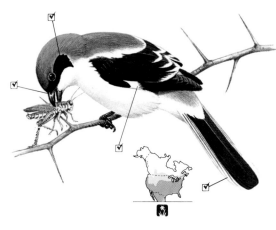

Loggerhead Shrike

Lanius ludovicianus

LENGTH:
7-9½ in.

WHAT TO LOOK FOR:
gray above, with black mask; paler below; bill short, heavy; wings black, with white patches; outer tail feathers white.

HABITAT:
open areas with scattered trees and shrubs.

Both the Loggerhead Shrike and the rarer Northern Shrike (*Lanius excubitor*) are nicknamed "butcher-birds." They kill insects, snakes, rodents, and small birds, then impale them on thorns or barbed wire or jam them into twig forks. Often they build up sizable larders. Evidently, however, the purpose of this habit is more than storage against lean times. For although the shrikes have hooked, hawklike bills, they lack powerful, hawklike feet and apparently must fix the prey on something firm before tearing it with the bill.

Northern Mockingbird

Mimus polyglottos

LENGTH:
9-11 in.

WHAT TO LOOK FOR:
gray above, whitish below; tail long, blackish; white wing patches; no black eye mask.

HABITAT:
open areas, farmland, suburbs, parks; scrubby growth near water (dry areas).

Gray Catbird

Dumetella carolinensis

LENGTH:
7-9 in.

WHAT TO LOOK FOR:
long tail; dark gray, with black cap and
rusty undertail.

HABITAT:
undergrowth in woodlands,
hedgerows, brushy areas, suburbs,
parks.

Often in the nesting season this trim
bird is a close neighbor of man. Like the mockingbird,
the Gray Catbird is regarded as a mimic, but it is less an
actual imitator than a plagiarist of musical ideas. As one listener put it, the catbird
"suggests the songs of various birds—never delivers the notes in their way!" It burbles
along, now loud, now soft, uttering a long run of squeaky phrases, seldom repeating
itself. It gets its name from its call note—a petulant, catlike mew.

◀ Northern Mockingbird (AT LEFT) Within its range the mockingbird is much more common
than the similarly colored shrikes. It is best known for its song, which may be heard day
or night. Typically the bird repeats a phrase over and over (perhaps half a dozen times),
then drops that phrase and goes on to another. Often the phrases are imitations of other
birds' songs, and "mockers" have also been known to sound like frogs, crickets, and
dogs, among others. They do not need a recent reminder, it seems, but can remember
phrases for several months at least.

Brown Thrasher

Toxostoma rufum

LENGTH: 9½-11 in.

WHAT TO LOOK FOR: long tail; bright reddish brown above; 2 white wingbars; white below, streaked with brown.

HABITAT: open brushy areas, forest edges, hedgerows, thickets, suburbs, parks.

Thrashers, like mockingbirds and catbirds, are members of the family Mimidae, or mimic thrushes. (The name thrasher derives from the word *thrush.*) A characteristic of this group is the imitation of sounds. The most notable quality of the thrasher's music, aside from the occasional imitation, is the phrasing. The loud, ringing song has been written in this vein: "*Hurry up, hurry up; plow it, plow it; harrow it; chuck; sow it, sow it, sow it; chuck-chuck, chuck-chuck; hoe it, hoe it.*" The bird is usually seen singing from a high perch out in the open.

Sage Thrasher

Oreoscoptes montanus

LENGTH: 8-9 in.

WHAT TO LOOK FOR: small thrasher; bill short, thin; gray-brown above, with 2 white wingbars; white below, streaked with brown; tail tipped with white.

HABITAT: shrubby areas, brushy slopes, sagebrush; deserts (winter).

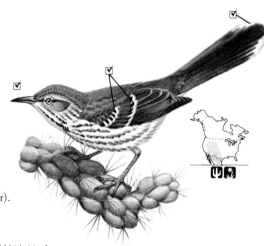

California Thrasher

Toxostoma redivivum

LENGTH:
11-13 in.

WHAT TO LOOK FOR:
bill long, curved down; long tail; dark gray-brown above, lighter below; cinnamon belly and undertail; dark mustache; light eye stripe.

HABITAT:
dry brushy areas, suburbs, parks.

Many birds that feed on the ground forage by scratching with their feet, kicking over leaves and other debris. But the California Thrasher uses its long, curved bill, uncovering hidden food and chopping deep into the earth after buried larvae. Its diet includes beetles, ants, bees, and caterpillars. Very strong afoot, this thrasher seems to prefer running to flying except in emergencies. Not all grayish, sickle-billed thrashers are necessarily this species. Three other somewhat similar thrashers are found in California and the Southwest: the Curve-billed (*Toxostoma curvirostre*), Le Conte's (*Toxostoma lecontei*), and the Crissal (*Toxostoma dorsale*).

◄ Sage Thrasher (AT LEFT) This small thrasher is a bird of the dry foothills and plains. It nests on the ground or, more usually, low down in sagebrush or other shrubby growth. Nest materials include twigs, plant stems, and bark fibers, with hair and fine roots for lining. Occasionally Sage Thrashers build a twig "awning" in the branches above the nest, as if to provide shade from the hot sun. Their song, a series of trills and warbles somewhat like that of the eastern Brown Thrasher, sounds more fluent because it lacks the pauses between the repeated phrases.

IMMATURE

American Robin
Turdus migratorius

LENGTH:
9-11 in.

WHAT TO LOOK FOR:
bright reddish orange below; dark gray above (head
paler on female), with broken eye ring and white-
tipped tail; immature with light, speckled breast.

HABITAT:
open forests, farmlands, suburbs, parks; sheltered
areas with fruit on trees (winter).

The Robin, a member of the thrush family, is one of the most neighborly
of birds. A pair will often build their nest—a neat cup of mud and grasses—
on a branch of a dooryard tree or on the ledge of a porch; and they hunt
confidently for earthworms on the lawn and in the garden, regardless of
human activities nearby. Robins eat insects as well as worms; they also like
fruits, both wild and cultivated.

MALE

FEMALE

Varied Thrush

Ixoreus naevius

LENGTH:
8-9½ in.

WHAT TO LOOK FOR:
dark gray above, with pale orange eye stripe and wingbars; orange below, with black breast band; female paler, browner, with gray breast band.

HABITAT:
damp coniferous and mixed forests, other moist woodlands, wooded canyons.

The Varied Thrush, though a native of the Pacific Northwest, is famous as a winter wanderer outside its normal range. The species has turned up in many unexpected places, frequently as far east as the Atlantic Coast. Even for a thrush, its song is remarkable. The singer makes use of a "scale" of five or six notes, and—choosing these pitches in no particular order—whistles a series of pure single notes, each note rising to a crescendo and then fading away to a brief pause.

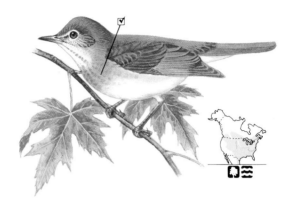

Veery

Catharus fuscescens

LENGTH:
6½-7½ in.

WHAT TO LOOK FOR:
brownish red above; whitish below, with buffy, brown-spotted breast band; in the West, darker and less reddish.

HABITAT:
humid deciduous woodlands, river groves, wooded swamps.

The name Veery is said to have been coined in imitation of the bird's song, a downward-spiraling series of hollow, liquid phrases best written as *whree-u, whree-u, whree-u,* and so on. Many thrushes—this one in particular—sing far into the dusk and sometimes even after dark. Veeries feed on the ground, hopping along and turning over dead leaves.

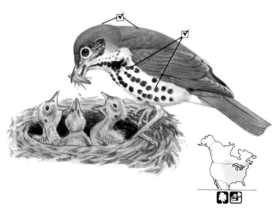

Wood Thrush

Hylocichla mustelina

LENGTH:
7½-8½ in.

WHAT TO LOOK FOR:
head and upper back reddish brown; white below, with large, dark brown spots from throat to belly.

HABITAT:
moist deciduous forests, suburbs, parks.

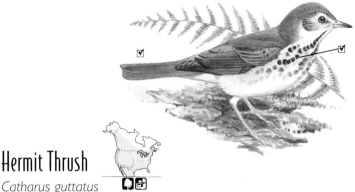

Hermit Thrush
Catharus guttatus

LENGTH:
6-7½ in.

WHAT TO LOOK FOR:
brown above, with reddish rump and tail; white below, with dark spots on throat and breast.

HABITAT:
moist coniferous or mixed forests; other woodlands, parks (migration).

The song of this retiring bird is an extraordinary sequence of phrases with varying pitches. Each phrase begins with a single whistle and closes with a jumble of brilliant, bubbly notes. On nesting territory in the northern forests, its song may often be heard with the songs of Swainson's and the Gray-cheeked Thrush (*Catharus ustulatus* and *minimus*), olive-backed birds that lack the Hermit's rusty tail.

◀ **Wood Thrush** (AT LEFT) This thrush nests in dark, damp woods, where it builds a tidy cup of grasses, stems, and dead leaves, usually mixed with mud and lined with roots. Often strips of birch bark, paper, or white cloth are woven into the structure. The Wood Thrush's song is complex and beautiful—a series of brief, liquid phrases often interspersed with a high trill.

FEMALE

MALE

Mountain Bluebird

Sialia currucoides

LENGTH:
6-7½ in.

WHAT TO LOOK FOR:
male sky-blue above, light blue below; female
mostly gray, with some blue; immature grayer,
with streaked underparts.

HABITAT:
open high-elevation areas with scattered trees and
brush; sometimes in lowlands.

Both the Eastern and the Western Bluebird (*Sialia mexicana*) hunt for insects by scan-
ning the ground from perches on wires or fence posts and then dropping on the prey.
The Mountain Bluebird, which eats a greater proportion of insects than the other two
do (seeds and berries are also part of the diet), does more of its hunting in the air. It
darts out from a perch to catch a flying insect, or flies over the ground and hovers, then
pounces. Like other bluebirds, this one nests in cavities, especially old woodpecker dig-
gings; it also uses birdhouses and holes in cliffs and banks.

Eastern Bluebird

Sialia sialis

LENGTH:
5-7 in.

WHAT TO LOOK FOR:
male bright blue above, with orange-red throat
and breast; female paler; immature mostly gray,
spotted with white on back and breast.

HABITAT:
open areas with scattered trees and fencerows;
farmlands, orchards, suburbs.

The sweet *chirrup* and the flash of blue in garden or orchard or along a rural road have
made the Eastern Bluebird a special favorite. But for many years this much-admired
bird has been in trouble; introduced House Sparrows and Starlings have taken over its
preferred tree holes. Fortunately, bluebirds will nest in birdhouses specially designed to
keep out the alien intruders. In many areas, hundreds of these houses have been set up
along "bluebird trails"—ambitious projects that have halted the species' decline and
even reversed it in some places.

FEMALE

MALE

MALE

Phainopepla

Phainopepla nitens

LENGTH:
6½-7½ in.

WHAT TO LOOK FOR:
crest; male glossy black, with white wing patches conspicuous in flight; female and immature dingy gray, with pale wing patches.

HABITAT:
scrubby arid and semiarid areas with scattered trees; oak groves in canyons.

The name Phainopepla means "shining robe," a reference to the bright, silky plumage of the male. The species is believed to be related to the waxwings, and like them it is both a fly catcher and a fruit eater. The Phainopepla's shallow nest, made of small twigs, sticky leaves and blossoms, and spiderwebs, is usually placed in a fork of a mesquite or other small tree. The male generally begins the project, and his mate does the rest of the job.

IMMATURE

Cedar Waxwing

Bombycilla cedrorum

LENGTH:
5½-7½ in.

WHAT TO LOOK FOR:
crest; mostly soft brown, with black face pattern, yellow-tipped tail, and red spots on wing; immature with brown streaks.

HABITAT:
open forests, areas with scattered trees, wooded swamps, orchards, suburbs.

Cedar Waxwings are a particularly sociable species. It is not unusual to see a row of them perched on a branch, passing a berry or an insect down the line and back again, bill to bill, in a ceremony that ends when one swallows the food. The birds wander in flocks whose arrivals and departures are unpredictable. Flocks of the northwestern Bohemian Waxwing (*Bombycilla garrulus*) are also erratic, and may suddenly appear well outside their normal range.

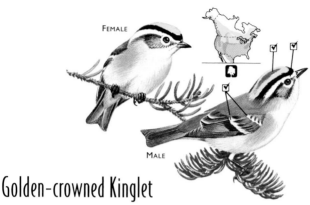

FEMALE

MALE

Golden-crowned Kinglet

Regulus satrapa

LENGTH:
3-4 in.

WHAT TO LOOK FOR:
small size; center of crown orange (male) or yellow (female); greenish above, with white eye stripe and wingbars.

HABITAT:
coniferous forests; other forests, thickets (migration, winter).

Restless, flitting movements and a very small size are good signs that the bird you are looking at is a kinglet. Scarcely pausing to perch, kinglets glean small insects and their eggs from leaves and bark. In its fluttering flight the Golden-crowned Kinglet utters a high, thin *sssst*, which is often repeated several times as a phrase.

Ruby-crowned Kinglet

Regulus calendula

LENGTH:
3½-4 in.

WHAT TO LOOK FOR:
small size; greenish above, with white eye ring and wingbars; red crown (male); often flicks wings.

HABITAT:
coniferous forests; other woodlands, thickets (migration, winter).

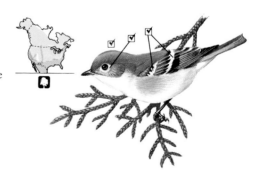

Blue-gray Gnatcatcher
Polioptila caerulea

LENGTH:
4-5 in.

WHAT TO LOOK FOR:
slim, long-tailed bird; blue-gray above, white below; tail blackish, with white outer feathers; white eye ring.

HABITAT:
mixed and oak forests, chaparral, open pinyon-juniper forests, thickets and groves along rivers.

This tiny bird darts from perch to perch, uttering its thin, mewing *spee,* flicking its long tail, and feeding on minute insects. In the breeding season the male has a soft, warbling song. He assists with the building of the nest, which may be located as low as 3 feet or as high as 80 feet above the ground. The structure is roughly the shape of an acorn with the top hollowed out, and it consists of various fine materials, including plant down, petals, feathers, and hair.

◀ Ruby-crowned Kinglet (AT LEFT) The ruby crown of this kinglet is worn only by the males, and even on them it is not always evident. (The amount of red that shows seems to depend on how agitated the kinglet is.) Though a mere mite of a bird, it has a loud and varied song, and ornithologists from Audubon on have mentioned how astonished they were the first time they heard a Ruby-crowned Kinglet sing.

Warbling Vireo

Vireo gilvus

LENGTH:
4½-5½ in.

WHAT TO LOOK FOR:
no conspicuous markings; gray-ish green above, white below.

HABITAT:
open mixed and deciduous forests; groves; orchards; shade trees in towns and suburbs.

Twelve species of vireos nest in North America. The Warbling Vireo and a few others have continent-wide ranges. Others—the eastern White-eyed (*Vireo griseus*) and western Bell's (*Vireo bellii*), for example—are limited to smaller areas. All are noted for the leisurely pace of their activity, compared with that of kinglets and warblers, with which they are often seen on migration. They also have thicker bills.

Solitary Vireo

Vireo solitarius

LENGTH:
4½-6 in.

WHAT TO LOOK FOR:
white "spectacles;" white wingbars; gray or bluish head; greenish or gray above, mostly white below.

HABITAT:
mixed or coniferous forests.

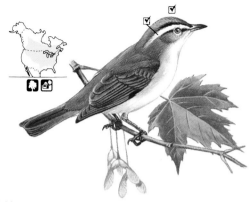

Red-eyed Vireo

Vireo olivaceus

LENGTH:
5-6½ in.

WHAT TO LOOK FOR:
white eye stripe; gray cap; greenish above, white below; no wingbars.

HABITAT:
deciduous woodlands, open areas with scattered trees, suburbs.

During the breeding season the male Red-eyed Vireo is a persistent singer, delivering lengthy passages of short, two- to six-note phrases. The bird tends to go on so long that he used to be nicknamed "preacher." Usually he sings at normal volume, but in courtship he also has a "whisper song," sometimes quite different in character from the regular song.

◀ **Solitary Vireo** (AT LEFT) Like all the vireos, the Solitary hangs its nest by the rim in a twiggy fork. As a structure too, the nest is typical of vireos, consisting of bits of bark and moss, leaves, and fine materials such as wool and feathers. The parents sing to each other as they share incubation and early care of the young. The song is bright and measured, not unlike a pure robin song.

Black-and-white Warbler

Mniotilta varia

LENGTH:
4-5½ in.

WHAT TO LOOK FOR:
streaked black and white above, white below; white stripe through crown; female and immature duller.

HABITAT: deciduous forests; parks, gardens with trees (migration).

Early ornithologists called this species the Black-and-white Creeper or Creeping Warbler. Constantly in motion, it searches for insects on bark, moving along head up like a creeper or down like a nuthatch. It has a brisk, sibilant song, usually a string of high-pitched double syllables—*weesee, weesee, weesee, weesee.*

Tennessee Warbler

Vermivora peregrina

LENGTH:
4-5 in.

WHAT TO LOOK FOR:
gray cap; white eye stripe; greenish above, white below; female and immature yellowish.

HABITAT:
open mixed and deciduous forests, brushy areas, forest edges.

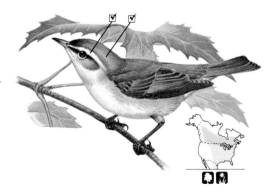

Northern Parula

Parula americana

LENGTH:
3½-4 in.

WHAT TO LOOK FOR:
blue above, with greenish-yellow patch on back; white wingbars; throat and breast yellow; darker band across throat (male).

HABITAT:
humid forests, usually near water; other forests (migration).

The name parula means "little titmouse," a reference to the bird's active behavior as it forages through the foliage for insects. In the South, the parula hollows out a shallow nest in trailing clumps of Spanish Moss; in northern forests, it nests in *Usnea* lichen. Its song is a buzzy trill, sliding upward in pitch and snapping off at the end—*zzzzzzzz-zup*.

◀ Tennessee Warbler (AT LEFT) The ornithologist Alexander Wilson discovered this species and the related Nashville Warbler (*Vermivora ruficapilla*) on an 1810 bird-finding trip in the South. Like many birds, these two were named for the places where they were first seen.

Prothonotary Warbler
Protonotaria citrea

LENGTH:
4½-5 in.

WHAT TO LOOK FOR:
bright orange-yellow head and breast, fading to lighter below; gray wings and tail; female more yellowish.

HABITAT:
wooded bottomlands; lowland swamps; moist, frequently flooded woods.

Court officers, or prothonotaries, who sometimes wore bright yellow robes, inspired the name of this handsome species. The Prothonotary Warbler is a bird of wooded swamps and riverbanks. As a rule it nests in a tree cavity or a deserted woodpecker hole, but in some localities it is tame enough to choose a birdhouse or any other small container.

American Redstart
Setophaga ruticilla

LENGTH:
4-5½ in.

WHAT TO LOOK FOR:
male black, with white belly and orangish patches on wings and tail; female and immature grayish above, white below, with yellow patches.

HABITAT:
second-growth deciduous forests, thickets, suburbs, parks.

FEMALE

MALE

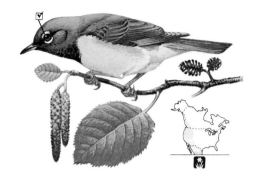

MacGillivray's Warbler

Oporornis tolmiei

LENGTH:
4½-5½ in.

WHAT TO LOOK FOR:
slate-gray head, blackish near breast; incomplete white eye ring; olive-green above, yellow below; female and immature duller.

HABITAT:
dense brushy areas, moist thickets.

Three warblers have gray hoods—this one, the similar Mourning Warbler (*Oporornis philadelphia*) of the North and East, and the Connecticut Warbler (*Oporornis agilis*), also a northern bird. All three skulk in dense vegetation near the ground. This species was named for a Scottish ornithologist who edited Audubon's writings.

◄ **American Redstart** (AT LEFT) One of the commonest warblers, this is also one of the most attractive. Flashes of color on the fanned-out wings and tail ("redstart" means "red-tailed") make the lively birds resemble flitting butterflies as they catch insects on the wing. The variable song is a set of single or double notes on one pitch, which may end with a higher or lower note—*zee-zee-zee-zee-zee-zeeo*.

Northern Waterthrush

Seiurus noveboracensis

LENGTH:
5-6 in.

WHAT TO LOOK FOR:
pale eye stripe; dark brown above, buffy with
dark streaks below; teeters continually.

HABITAT:
wet woodlands; brushy areas (migration).

Look and listen for this warbler near placid water. The closely related
Louisiana Waterthrush (*Seiurus motacilla*) is more likely near fast-flowing
streams. Both species bob and teeter along over banks, rocks, and logs. Their
looks are similar, but with practice they can be distinguished by their voices.
Both build their nests, of moss and other bits of vegetation, near water.

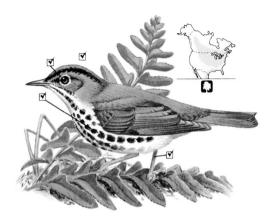

Ovenbird

Seiurus aurocapillus

LENGTH:
5-6 in.

WHAT TO LOOK FOR:
olive above, with orange crown bordered by black; white below, with dark streaks; white eye ring; pinkish legs; walks on ground.

HABITAT:
deciduous woodlands.

Once it has become familiar, the voice of the Ovenbird is one of the most obvious in the woods. The song begins softly and builds to a ringing crescendo—*teacher, teacher, teacher, teacher!* The Ovenbird is a ground dwelling warbler. Its covered nest, which accounts for its name, is generally hidden on the forest floor.

Warblers *Wilsonia*

Identifying Warblers. North America has more than 50 species of warblers, distinguished as a group by their small size, thin, sharp bills, active behavior, and bright or contrasting colors in spring. Warblers are usually dimorphic—that is, the sexes differ in plumage. In general, female warblers are paler and duller, lacking the distinctive markings of the males. In the fall many males lose most of these identifying marks; they become as drab as the females, and immature birds looking somewhat like adult females add to the confusion. Unless otherwise noted, all warblers shown in this book are males in breeding plumage.

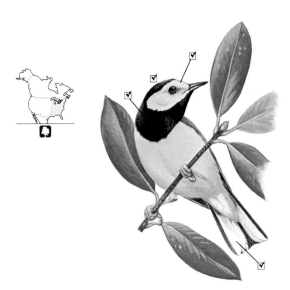

Hooded Warbler

Wilsonia citrina

LENGTH :
4¼-5½ in.

WHAT TO LOOK FOR:
male with yellow face, black hood, black throat; female with brownish cap; greenish above, yellow below; white on tail.

HABITAT:
dense deciduous forests, wooded swamps, thickets; usually near water.

In the East two common warblers have black caps on yellow heads. One is this species; the other is Wilson's Warbler (*Wilsonia pusilla*), which ranges the continent and lacks the Hooded's black bib. The Hooded Warbler is a bird of the undergrowth, nesting low in a bush or sapling. From the outside the nest looks like a wad of dead leaves, but inside it is an impressive construction of bark, plant fibers, down, grass, and spiderweb.

Canada Warbler

Wilsonia canadensis

LENGTH:
4½-5½ in.

WHAT TO LOOK FOR:
gray above, yellow below; "spectacles"; male
with black "necklace"; female duller, with faint
"necklace."

HABITAT:
mature deciduous woodlands near streams or
swamps; moist brushy areas; second-growth
forests (migration).

This distinctively marked species breeds in cool, damp forests in Canada and
elsewhere. It is usually a ground-nester, frequently choosing a site in or near
a moss-covered log or stump. Its song is a bright, rapid warble on one pitch.

MALE

FEMALE

Common Yellowthroat

Geothlypis trichas

LENGTH:
4-5½ in.

WHAT TO LOOK FOR:
male with black mask, edged above with white; greenish brown above, with yellow throat, upper breast, and undertail; female without mask.

HABITAT:
wet brushy areas, freshwater and saltwater marshes.

This familiar warbler, black-masked like a little bandit, is usually first seen peering at the intruder from the depths of a shrub or thicket. Sooner or later, the Yellowthroat announces itself with a rhythmic *witchery, witchery, witchery* or variations on that theme. Yellowthroats sometimes nest in loose colonies, but most often breeding pairs are well distributed through brushy or marshy areas.

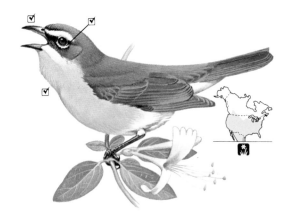

Yellow-breasted Chat

Icteria virens

LENGTH:
6½-7½ in.

WHAT TO LOOK FOR:
largest warbler; dark mask; heavy bill; white "spectacles;" green above; yellow breast.

HABITAT:
dense thickets and tangles, usually near water; shrubby areas in upland pastures.

For years ornithologists have been saying that this bird is in all probability not really a warbler. It is half again as big as some species, and much more robust. Its song is loud and varied. One observer who tried to put a passage into syllables got this result "*C-r-r-r-r-r—whirr—that's it—chee—quack, cluck—yit-yit-yit—now hit it—tr-r-r—when—caw, caw—cut, cut—tea-boy—who, who—mew, mew—*and so on till you are tired of listening."

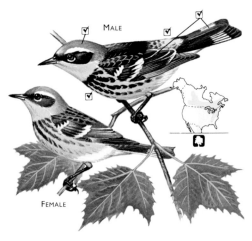

MALE

FEMALE

Magnolia Warbler

Dendroica magnolia

LENGTH:
4-5 in.

WHAT TO LOOK FOR:
black above, yellow streaked with black below; gray cap; yellow rump; wings and tail black, with large white patches; female and immature paler.

HABITAT:
coniferous forests; other wooded areas (migration).

Alexander Wilson first sighted this warbler in magnolia trees, and the scientific name he gave it included the word magnolia. Eventually "Magnolia Warbler," being a pretty way of referring to a beautiful bird, became the common name. But as one authority remarked, if the warbler had to be named after a tree, spruce or balsam would have been more appropriate for this northern forest bird.

Palm Warbler

Dendroica palmarum

LENGTH:
4-5½ in.

WHAT TO LOOK FOR:
reddish cap (breeding); underparts yellow or whitish, streaked, with yellow undertail; wags tail.

HABITAT:
forest swamps, bogs; brushy areas (migration, winter).

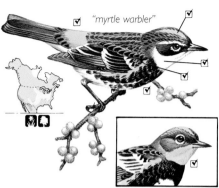
"myrtle warbler"

"Audubon's warbler"

Yellow-rumped Warbler
Dendroica coronata

LENGTH:
4½-5½ in.

WHAT TO LOOK FOR:
male with yellow crown, rump, and shoulder patch, white (East) or yellow (West) throat, black bib, white tail patches (visible mainly in flight); female and immature paler, browner.

HABITAT:
coniferous and mixed forests; other woodlands, thickets (migration, winter).

This is one of the most abundant of our warblers, and at times in migration seems to outnumber all the others combined. It has a bright, loud chip call that is easily learned, but recognizing its trilling song takes practice. Audubon's Warbler (the western subspecies) and the eastern Myrtle were long considered separate species.

◄ **Palm Warbler** (AT LEFT) Ornithologists first observed this warbler wintering among the palms of Florida, hence its common name—surely a misnomer for a species breeding in northern bogs. During migration the Palm Warbler is often seen on the ground or in a low tree, where it flicks its tail up and down. The Prairie Warbler (*Dendroica discolor*), common in areas crossed by migrating Palms, flicks its tail from side to side. It lacks the red cap and yellow undertail.

Black-throated Green Warbler

Dendroica virens

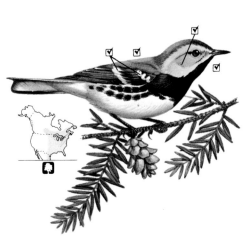

LENGTH:
4-5 in.

WHAT TO LOOK FOR:
yellow face; black throat and breast; green above; white wing-bars; female and immature duller, with less black.

HABITAT:
coniferous forests; other woodlands (migration, winter).

The Black-throated Green has a preference for pines and other conifers, but during migration it can be seen high up in a deciduous tree or low down in a roadside thicket. This is the only eastern warbler with yellowish cheeks. Other handsome, similar-looking species are Townsend's Warbler (*Dendroica townsendi*) and the Hermit Warbler (*Dendroica occidentalis*), both of the Far West.

Yellow Warbler

Dendroica petechia

LENGTH:
4-5 in.

WHAT TO LOOK FOR:
mostly yellow (more greenish above); male streaked with reddish on breast; female duller.

HABITAT:
riverside woodlands, wet thickets, brushy marsh edges, orchards, suburbs, parks.

FEMALE

MALE

Black-throated Gray Warbler

Dendroica nigrescens

LENGTH:
4-5 in.

WHAT TO LOOK FOR:
male with black head and throat, white stripe above and below eye; gray above, white below; female and immature paler, with less black.

HABITAT:
oak, juniper, and pinyon forests, mixed woodlands with heavy undergrowth.

Like a number of other *Dendroica* warblers, this species is partial to evergreen trees, at least in the mountains of the Northwest. Farther south, it breeds in the dry scrubby growth of canyon and valley walls. Its nests are not easy to find; they are often located, for example, at the junction of several leafy twigs that hold and screen the structure.

◀ Yellow Warbler (AT LEFT) This species has the largest breeding range of any warbler and is common not only in most of North America but as far south as Peru. The Yellow Warbler often nests in willows, alders, or other shrubs along the edge of a swamp or road; its neat cup of silvery plant fibers is usually built in a low fork. The male is a persistent singer with two basic songs: *pip-pip-pip-sissewa-is sweet* and *wee-see-wee-see-wiss-wiss-u.*

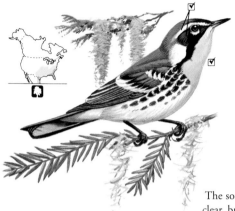

Yellow-throated Warbler
Dendroica dominica

LENGTH:
5-5½ in.

WHAT TO LOOK FOR:
yellow throat; gray above; black and white pattern on face; female similar but duller.

HABITAT:
pine and oak forests, cypress swamps.

The song of the Yellow-throated Warbler is a clear, bright whistle—*see-wee, see-wee, see-wee, swee, swee, swee, swee*—that speeds up and drops in pitch toward the end. This bird seems less nervous than many other warblers. It forages carefully for insects on tree bark in much the manner of the Brown Creeper or the Black-and-white Warbler.

Black-throated Blue Warbler
Dendroica caerulescens

LENGTH
5-5½ in.

WHAT TO LOOK FOR:
male dark blue above, with prominent white wing spot and black face, throat, and sides; female dull olive (paler below), with white wing spot.

HABITAT:
deciduous and mixed forests with heavy undergrowth.

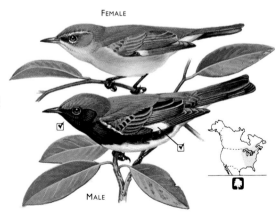

FEMALE

MALE

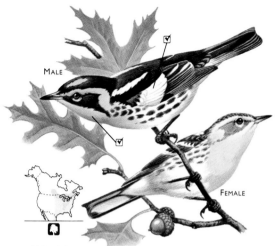

MALE

FEMALE

Blackburnian Warbler

Dendroica fusca

LENGTH:
4-5½ in.

WHAT TO LOOK FOR:
male with bright orange throat, striped black back, broad white wingbars; female and immature paler, brownish; facial pattern always present.

HABITAT:
coniferous or mixed forests; other woodlands (migration).

A bird of the deep woods, the Blackburnian nests in a variety of conifers—spruces, firs, pines, hemlocks. On migration it is a treetop forager and singer, often difficult to spot despite the glowing orange throat. Its song is thin and buzzy, ending with a single high, up-sliding note. The species was named for Anna Blackburn, an 18th-century patron of ornithology.

◀ Black-throated Blue Warbler (AT LEFT) The male Black-throated Blue looks the same in spring, summer, and fall, and so it is one of the easiest warblers to recognize. It is easy to spot, too, for it is usually found quite low in rhododendron, laurel, and similar undergrowth. To spot another blue-backed species, the Cerulean Warbler (*Dendroica cerulea*), observers may need to do a lot of neck-craning, since it usually feeds high in a tree.

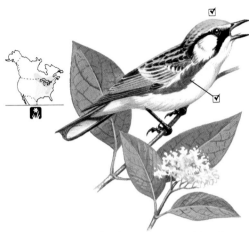

Chestnut-sided Warbler
Dendroica pensylvanica

LENGTH:
4-5 in.

WHAT TO LOOK FOR:
male with yellow cap and chestnut sides, whitish below; female duller, with spotty chestnut areas; immature yellowish green above, white below.

HABITAT:
brushy fields, open woodlands, farmlands.

The distinctive song of the Chestnut-sided Warbler helps to locate the bird. The usual version approximates *tsee, see, see, see, see, swee-BEAT-chew*, with the last note dropping in pitch; several generations of birders have used the words "I wish to see Miss Beecher" as a memory aid. The Bay-breasted Warbler (*Dendroica castanea*) is more richly colored, with deep chestnut on head, breast, and sides.

Pine Warbler
Dendroica pinus

LENGTH:
5-5½ in.

WHAT TO LOOK FOR:
olive-green above, yellowish with streaks below; white wingbars; female duller.

HABITAT:
open pine forests; deciduous woodlands (migration).

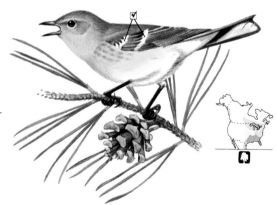

Blackpoll Warbler

Dendroica striata

LENGTH:
4¼-5½ in.

WHAT TO LOOK FOR:
male with black cap, white face,
black-streaked flanks; female
browner, without cap; in fall
both sexes greenish, with white
wingbars.

HABITAT:
coniferous woodlands; other
woodlands (migration).

Many birders greet the Blackpolls' arrival each
spring with some regret, for it signals the end of the exciting warbler
migration. The Blackpoll's song is said to be the highest in pitch of
any songbird's (some people can't hear it at all). It is a fast series of single syllables more or less on the same thin note, loudest in the middle.

◀ Pine Warbler (AT LEFT) The name of this bird is quite
appropriate; except when on migration, the Pine Warbler
"sticks to pine woods as a cockle-bur sticks to a dog's
tail." The nest is usually built in a clump of pine needles
or on the top of a pine bough between 15 and 80 feet
from the ground. The song is a loose, sweet trill.

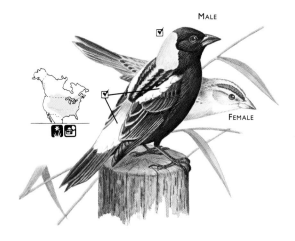

MALE

FEMALE

Bobolink

Dolichonyx oryzivorus

LENGTH:
5½-7½ in.

WHAT TO LOOK FOR:
breeding male black, with back of head yellowish and much white on wings and lower back; other plumages buffy, heavily streaked above.

HABITAT:
moist open fields, meadows, farmlands, marshes.

The jumbled tinkling of the Bobolink's song seems to come from every quarter of the wet meadow or grainfield where the bird nests. The male may be sitting on a weed stalk or fence post or in a tree along the edge; he may be hovering on beating wings or dashing after a female in courtship. Once the breeding season is over, the singing mostly ceases. The male molts into a plumage like that of his mate, and flocks of Bobolinks fly to South America, calling *pink* from time to time as they go.

WESTERN MEADOWLARK   EASTERN MEADOWLARK

Western Meadowlark

Sturnella neglecta

LENGTH:
8-10½ in.

WHAT TO LOOK FOR:
black V across bright yellow underparts; outer tail feathers white; streaked brown above.

HABITAT:
prairies, meadows, open areas.

Lewis and Clark first noticed the differences between this species and the Eastern Meadowlark (*Sturnella magna*), which look much alike but differ greatly in song. When Audubon rediscovered the Western Meadowlark in 1843, the scientific name he gave it poked fun at the long time between sightings: it means "neglected meadowlark." Many who have heard the songs of both meadowlarks believe that the sweet, melancholy phrases of the eastern bird cannot compare with the rich, flutelike bubbling of the western.

MALE

FEMALE

Red-winged Blackbird

Agelaius phoeniceus

LENGTH:
7-9½ in.

WHAT TO LOOK FOR:
male black, with yellow-bordered red shoulder patch; female dark brown, heavily streaked; immature male like female but with red patch.

HABITAT:
swamps, marshes, adjacent open areas, farmlands.

The male Red-winged Blackbird's song is a herald of spring. *Con-ka-ree*, he calls, as if proclaiming victory over winter. Red-wings feed and roost in flocks, but in late summer the flocks vanish. They have retired to some marsh, where the birds hide in the vegetation, molt their flight feathers, and grow new ones. Then the flocks reappear, headed south.

Brown-headed Cowbird

Molothrus ater

LENGTH:
6-8 in.

WHAT TO LOOK FOR:
conical bill; male glossy black, with dark brown head; female gray, with paler throat.

HABITAT:
farmlands, groves, forest edges, river woodlands.

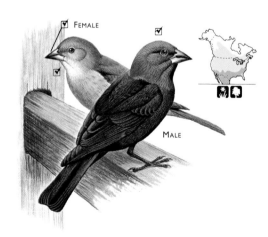

FEMALE

MALE

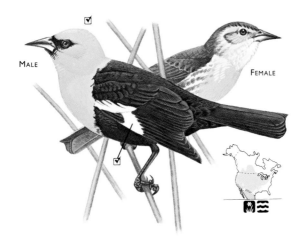

MALE

FEMALE

Yellow-headed Blackbird

Xanthocephalus xanthocephalus

LENGTH:
8-10 in.

WHAT TO LOOK FOR:
male black, with yellow head and breast and white wing patches; female brown, with dull yellow on face and breast and white throat.

HABITAT:
freshwater marshes, adjacent open areas.

This handsome species nests over water 2 to 4 feet deep, and may abandon a nest if the water level drops. The nests are slung between reed stems and are woven of soggy blades of dead grass. When the grass dries, the nest fabric tightens and the reeds are drawn together, improving the nest's stability. The lining is of leaves, grass, and filmy reed plumes.

◀ **Brown-headed Cowbird** (AT LEFT) Few birds are as generally disapproved of as the Brown-headed Cowbird, which lays its eggs in the nests of other birds, particularly flycatchers, sparrows, vireos, and warblers. A newly hatched cowbird quickly grows larger than the rightful nestlings and devours most of the food; it may even push the hosts' eggs or young out of the nest The foster parents feed the huge intruder until it can fly.

Common Grackle

Quiscalus quiscula

LENGTH:
10-12½ in.

WHAT TO LOOK FOR:
long keel-shaped tail; long pointed bill; light yellow eye; male glossy black, with purple, bronze, or greenish cast; female less glossy.

HABITAT:
farmlands, groves, suburbs, parks; usually near water.

Before the trees have begun to leaf out in the North, the Common Grackles arrive. Soon courting males are posturing in the treetops, puffing up their glossy plumage, spreading their long tails, and uttering their rasping *chu-seeck*. Larger species of grackles are the Great-tailed (*Quiscalus mexicanus*) of southern farmlands and the Boat-tailed (*Quiscalus major*), a salt-marsh bird.

NONBREEDING

BREEDING

European Starling

Sturnus vulgaris

LENGTH:
7-8½ in.

WHAT TO LOOK FOR:
long pointed bill; short, square tail; black overall, with greenish and purple gloss (nonbreeding with light spots); immature brownish, darker above.

HABITAT:
farmlands, open woodlands, brushy areas, towns, cities.

Brewer's Blackbird

Euphagus cyanocephalus

LENGTH:
7½-9½ in.

WHAT TO LOOK FOR:
male black, with yellow eye
and purple gloss on head;
female grayish brown, darker
above, with dark eye; tail proportionately shorter than grackle's.

HABITAT:
open areas, lakeshores.

FEMALE

MALE

Two medium-sized blackbirds closely resemble one another—
this species and the Rusty Blackbird (*Euphagus carolinus*). In winter they may be
found in many of the same regions, but Brewer's Blackbird frequents grassy areas
and the Rusty Blackbird swampy woods. Brewer's gives a strong rough whistle or a
"whirring gurgle"; the Rusty calls *tickle-EE*, sounding like a mechanical joint that
needs oiling.

◀ European Starling (AT LEFT) In 1890 the
efforts to introduce this European bird to
North America succeeded, and descen-
dants of the 100 birds released in New
York City began to spread across the land.
The starling's habit of gathering in huge
roosts has made it a pest in many areas,
and it deprives many hole-nesting species
of their homes. It does, however, eat many
destructive insects.

Baltimore/ Bullock's Oriole

Icterus galbula
Icterus bullockii

LENGTH:
6-7½ in.

WHAT TO LOOK FOR:
pointed bill; male orange, with black on head, throat, back, wings, and tail; female and immature pale yellow or orange below, brownish above, with white wingbars.

HABITAT:
open deciduous woodlands; shade trees in farmlands, towns, cities.

MALE BALTIMORE

FEMALE BALTIMORE

MALE BULLOCK'S

A liquid, whistled song and a flash of color at the top of a tall tree signal the presence of an oriole. Scientists have recently returned these orioles to two species, having merged them in the 1950s. Where the eastern Baltimore and western Bullock's ranges overlap in mid-continent there is some interbreeding, but not enough to consider them valid species. The Baltimore's nest is the familiar deep pouch swinging at the end of a slender limb; its western cousin's is often tied to twigs at the top and sides.

Orchard Oriole

Icterus spurius

LENGTH: 6½-7 in.

WHAT TO LOOK FOR:
adult male rusty brown, with black head, throat, upper breast, and upper back and black on wings and tail; first-year male greenish, with black throat; female yellowish green, darker above, with white wingbars.

HABITAT:
farmlands, orchards, suburbs, towns.

FEMALE

FIRST YEAR MALE

MALE

MALE

FEMALE

Scott's Oriole

Icterus parisorum

LENGTH
6½-8 in.

WHAT TO LOOK FOR:
male bright yellow, with black head, upper back, and throat and black on wings and tail; female and immature yellowish green, darker above, with whitish wingbars.

HABITAT:
deserts; semiarid areas; dry mountain slopes with oaks, pinyons, yucca.

Like other orioles, this western species feeds on insects, fruits, and probably nectar. Like its relatives, it sings throughout the day in the breeding season. And its nest, like theirs, is woven of plant fibers. Often hidden among the spiky dead leaves of a yucca, the nest varies in structure according to the surroundings.

◀ Orchard Oriole (AT LEFT) This bird does nest in orchards, where its preference for insects makes it particularly valuable, but it also nests in other habitats. An unusual site was discovered in Louisiana, where nests woven of salt-meadow grasses were suspended from canes in a marsh. The species often seems colonial. On one 7-acre plot in the Mississippi Delta, 114 orchard oriole nests were found in one season. Nearly 20 nests at a time have been noted in a single Louisiana Live Oak.

Scarlet Tanager
Piranga olivacea

LENGTH:
6-7 in.

WHAT TO LOOK FOR:
male scarlet, with black wings and tail (in fall, red replaced by yellowish green); female yellowish green, with darker wings and tail.

HABITAT:
thick deciduous woodlands, suburbs, parks.

The Scarlet Tanager's song is not hard to pick out; listen to a robin sing for a while, then listen for the same song with a burr in it. The species also has a distinctive, hoarse call—*chick-kurr* in the East, sometimes *chip-chiree* elsewhere. Scarlet Tanagers devour many destructive caterpillars and wood-boring beetles, most often but not exclusively in oaks. Young males may be principally orange or splotched with red and yellow.

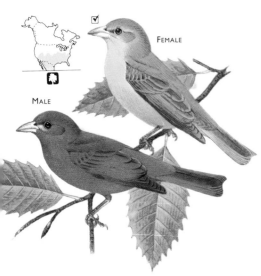

Summer Tanager
Piranga rubra

LENGTH:
6-7½ in.

WHAT TO LOOK FOR:
yellowish bill; male red; female yellowish green above, yellow below.

HABITAT:
woodlands; in uplands, drier forests of oak, hickory, or pine.

Western Tanager

Piranga ludoviciana

FEMALE

MALE

LENGTH:
6-7 in.

WHAT TO LOOK FOR:
male bright yellow, with red head and black on upper back, wings, and tail (no red on nonbreeder); female greenish above, yellowish below (only female tanager with wingbars).

HABITAT:
open mixed and coniferous woodlands; other forests (migration).

The song of the Western Tanager is much the same as that of the Scarlet Tanager—a series of short phrases separated by pauses. Its call is two- or three-syllabled—*pit-ic, pit-it-ic*. On migration, flocks of Western Tanagers pass through valleys, plains, and foothills. They nest mostly in the mountains, in firs and pines, often at high elevations. Like other tanagers, they lay three to five eggs. The female alone incubates, but both parents share the care and feeding of the nestlings.

◀ **Summer Tanager** (AT LEFT) Tanagers are mainly insect eaters, though they do take some buds and fruits. The Summer Tanager is especially fond of beetles and bees, and it will tear wasps' nests apart to get at the larvae. The hard parts of beetles are not digested, but are coughed up as pellets. This species builds a flimsy nest on a horizontal bough. Its song is a more musical version of the Scarlet Tanager's, and its spluttery call is traditionally written as *chicky-tucky-tuck.* A less common species, similar in appearance but with a dark mask, is the Hepatic Tanager (*Piranga flava*) of the mountainous Southwest.

Northern Cardinal

Cardinalis cardinalis

LENGTH:
7-8½ in.

WHAT TO LOOK FOR:
prominent crest; conical reddish bill; male bright red, with black around eye and bill; female brownish yellow, with red on wings and tail.

HABITAT:
open woods, forest edges, thickets, suburbs, parks.

FEMALE

MALE

The cardinal's rich coloring and its readiness to come to feeders have made it a favorite among bird-watchers. Its varied musical repertoire consists of loud, clear whistles that are usually repeated several times—*wheet, wheet, wheet, wheet, chew, chew, chew, cheedle, cheedle, cheedle.* Male and female may sing alternately, as if in response to each other. Cardinals also have a metallic *pink* note. This species is one of a number of southern birds that have extended their ranges northward during this century. Among the others are the Mockingbird, Tufted Titmouse, Turkey Vulture, and Red-bellied Woodpecker.

Blue Grosbeak

Guiraca caerulea

LENGTH:
6-7 in.

WHAT TO LOOK FOR:
large conical bill; rusty or buffy wingbars; male blue; female brownish, with dark wings.

HABITAT:
brushy areas, open woodlands, forests near rivers.

MALE

FEMALE

Evening Grosbeak
Coccothraustes vespertinus

LENGTH:
7-8 in.

WHAT TO LOOK FOR:
bill large, light-colored, conical; male yellow-brown, with black tail and black and white wings; female paler, grayish.

HABITAT:
coniferous forests; other forests and at feeders (migration, winter).

The Evening Grosbeak was given its name by an observer who heard a flock at twilight, at a site northwest of Lake Superior. At that time—1823—the Evening Grosbeak was a western species; since then, it has spread far to the east. One hypothesis is that feeding trays loaded with sunflower seeds may have played a part in this expansion, but reports show that grosbeaks regularly pass up such offerings in favor of boxelder seeds and other wild food.

◀ Blue Grosbeak (AT LEFT) Snakeskins are occasionally woven into the nest of the Blue Grosbeak, sometimes covering the entire outside; other nesting materials include dry leaves, cornhusks, and strips of plastic or newspaper. The female incubates the four eggs for 11 days; the young—fed by both parents, mostly on insects and snails—leave the nest less than two weeks after hatching. For adults, fruits, seeds, and other vegetable matter make up perhaps a third of the diet.

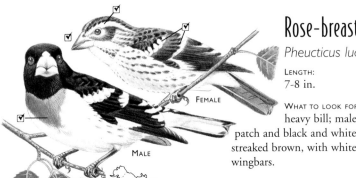

Rose-breasted Grosbeak

Pheucticus ludovicianus

LENGTH:
7-8 in.

WHAT TO LOOK FOR:
heavy bill; male with rose breast patch and black and white pattern; female streaked brown, with white eye stripe and wingbars.

HABITAT:
deciduous woodlands, groves, suburbs.

Conspicuous in his showy plumage, the male Rose-breasted Grosbeak joins the spring chorus in April or early May. His song has a cheery, lyrical quality, with almost the swing of a march. Though the less colorful female is usually the one to build the loosely constructed nest, some pairs will share the work and both male and female incubate. If a pair raises a second brood, the male may take charge of the first while his mate sits on the new eggs.

Indigo Bunting

Passerina cyanea

LENGTH:
4½-5½ in.

WHAT TO LOOK FOR:
male indigo-blue, with blackish wings and tail, no wingbars; female brown above, whitish below, with faint streaking on breast.

HABITAT:
brushy areas, scrubby fields, forest edges.

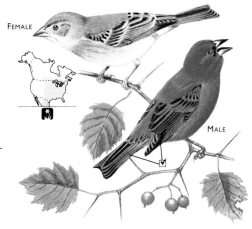

The male Indigo Bunting is one of the few birds giving full-voiced performances at midday. A typical song has been written down as *sir, chewe, chewe, cheer, cheer, swe, swe, chir, chir chir, sir, sir, see, see, fish, fish, fish.* The western Lazuli Bunting (*Passerina amoena*), with sky-blue head, rusty breast, and wingbars, interbreeds with the Indigo where their ranges overlap.

MALE · FEMALE

Black-headed Grosbeak

Pheucticus melanocephalus

LENGTH:
6½-7½ in.

WHAT TO LOOK FOR:
heavy whitish bill; male orangish yellow, with black head and black and white wings; female brownish, with facial pattern and streaks.

HABITAT:
open mixed or deciduous woodlands, forest edges, chaparral, orchards, parks.

This species is the western counterpart of the Rose-breasted Grosbeak, and their clear, whistled songs are similar. The usual song of the Black-headed Grosbeak lasts about five seconds, but may be longer; a male once performed for seven hours.

Painted Bunting

Passerina ciris

LENGTH:
5-5½ in.

WHAT TO LOOK FOR:
male with blue head, red underparts and rump, and green back; female green above, yellowish below.

HABITAT:
brushy fields, forest edges, shrubby streamsides, fencerows, towns.

MALE

FEMALE

Considered by many to be North America's most beautifully colored bird, the male Painted Bunting justly merits the nickname "nonpareil" (unequaled). Males are very conspicuous as they sing from high, exposed perches, but the species favors thick ground cover and shrubbery for feeding and nesting. The majority of Painted Buntings migrate to Central America, though some may overwinter in Florida.

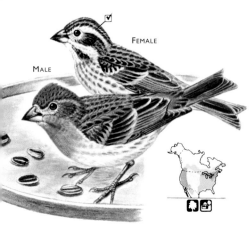

Purple Finch
Carpodacus purpureus

LENGTH:
5¼-6 in.

WHAT TO LOOK FOR:
male with white belly and raspberry-red head, upperparts, and breast; female brown above, heavily streaked below, with broad white stripe behind eye.

HABITAT:
mixed woodlands, suburbs, and at feeders (migration, winter).

These handsome finches move erratically from place to place, often in large numbers. In winter an area with few or no Purple Finches one day may have thousands the next. Flocks may consist mostly or solely of brightly colored males or of brown females and immatures. In late summer Purple Finches begin to molt, and in winter plumage the males' reddish areas appear frosted. With wear, the whitish tinge disappears, revealing the rich breeding color.

Red Crossbill
Loxia curvirostra

LENGTH:
5½-6 in.

WHAT TO LOOK FOR:
crossed tips of bill; male brick-red, with dark wings and tail; female greenish yellow, lighter below.

HABITAT:
coniferous forests; occasionally in other woodlands.

House Finch

Carpodacus mexicanus

FEMALE
MALE

LENGTH:
5-5½ in.

WHAT TO LOOK FOR:
male with bright red head, breast, and
rump; female dull brown, with faintly
streaked breast and no eye stripe.

HABITAT:
deserts, scrubby areas, open forests, farmlands,
towns, suburbs; at feeders.

The House Finch is an exceptionally adaptable species. Once
restricted to the Southwest, it began to extend its range in the
1920s; following the release of caged birds in New York in 1940,
House Finches spread in the East. The birds nest in all sorts of
sites—in holes in trees, among cactus spines, on the beams of
buildings, and in the nests of other birds. In the West, Cassin's
Finch (*Carpodacus cassinii*) may be mistaken for this species or for
the Purple Finch.

◀ Red Crossbill (AT LEFT) The two crossbills—the Red and the White-
winged (*Loxia leucoptera*)—are nomads, following the seed crops of
conifers or sometimes other forest trees. Their choice of when to nest
also seems to depend on the cone supply; they will nest in early spring
or even late winter if food is plentiful. A crossbill uses its beak to pry
apart the scales of a cone while the tongue extracts the seeds.

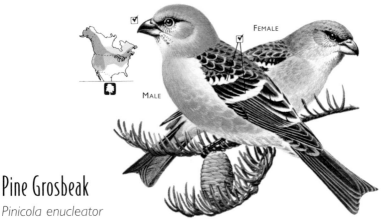

Pine Grosbeak

Pinicola enucleator

LENGTH:
7½-9½ in.

WHAT TO LOOK FOR:
large size; conical blackish bill; white wingbars; male mostly rosy red, with blackish wings and tail; female greenish brown above, grayer below.

HABITAT:
coniferous forests; other woodlands (some winters).

The scientific name of this species translates roughly as "the bird that lives in pines and shells the seeds." But the Pine Grosbeak has a far more varied diet than the name implies—one that includes beechnuts, crab apples, weed seeds, and insects. Pine Grosbeaks breed in the Far North and in mountain areas. In winter they fly to lower latitudes and elevations.

Common Redpoll

Carduelis flammea

LENGTH:
4½-5½ in.

WHAT TO LOOK FOR:
red forehead; black chin; streaked back and sides; white wingbars; breast and rump pinkish (male).

HABITAT:
scrub forests, tundra; brushy areas, birch groves, and at feeders (winter).

NONBREEDING MALE

FEMALE

MALE

American Goldfinch

Carduelis tristis

LENGTH:
4-5 in.

WHAT TO LOOK FOR:
male bright yellow, with black forehead, wings, and tail; female olive-green above, lighter below; white rump; both sexes yellowish brown in winter; undulating flight.

HABITAT:
farmlands, weedy fields with scattered trees, river groves, suburbs, parks, at feeders.

Goldfinches breed late in the summer, when thistledown is available for their tightly woven nests. Feeding flocks can be located by their song, chirps interspersed with *swe-si-iees* or *per-chick-o-rees,* which they also utter in flight. In the West is the Lesser Goldfinch (*Carduelis psaltria*), with a dark back.

◀ Common Redpoll (AT LEFT) These northern-breeding "winter finches" occasionally appear at feeders farther south. But often redpolls are much more secretive; they chatter high overhead, become visible for an instant as they dive for a thicket, and then vanish. The Pine Siskin (*Carduelis pinus*), which flocks with redpolls, has yellow on the wings and tail and no red anywhere.

EASTERN
FEMALE

EASTERN
MALE

SPOTTED
MALE

Eastern/Spotted Towhee

Pipilo erythrophthalmus
Pipilo maculatus

LENGTH:
7-8 in.

WHAT TO LOOK FOR:
male mostly black and white, with rufous flanks and white on wings and tail; white spots on back (Spotted); female with brown instead of black.

HABITAT:
thickets, open forests, brushy fields, chaparral, suburbs, parks.

A loud, buzzy *shree* or *shrank* from the underbrush and vigorous scratching in the leaves announce the presence of an Eastern Towhee. Its song is often transcribed as *drink-your-teeeee*. In the West, the Spotted Towhee behaves much the same, and it sounds much like its eastern cousin. There are other towhee species in the West; the California (*Pipilo crissalis*) and the Canyon (*Pipilo fuscus*) were once considered one species. They are common in suburban yards.

MALE

FEMALE

Lark Bunting
Calamospiza melanocorys

LENGTH:
5½-7 in.

WHAT TO LOOK FOR:
male black or dark gray, with large white wing patch; female, immature, and winter male brown above, finely streaked below, with light wing patch.

HABITAT:
prairies, semiarid areas, brushy fields.

Lark Buntings are gregarious. They winter and travel in flocks, and nest fairly close together. The conspicuously marked breeding males perform song flights in which they rise more or less straight up to a height of 10 to 30 feet and then rock slowly down with stiff wings, butterfly-fashion, singing from start to landing. Often several will do this together.

Savannah Sparrow

Passserculus sandwichensis

LENGTH:
4-6 in.

WHAT TO LOOK FOR:
streaked above, heavily streaked below; light stripe above eye; short tail; varies from pale to dark.

HABITAT:
tundra, prairies, meadows, salt marshes, beaches.

When alarmed, the Savannah Sparrow seems to prefer running through the grass to flying. When it does fly up it usually skims over the grass very briefly, then drops out of sight. Males often sing from a weed-top perch. The song—*tsip-tsip-tsip-seeeee-saaaaay*—ends in a two-part trill that at a distance is all that can be heard. "Savannah" is a fair description of the bird's habitat, but the name actually refers to the Georgia city where the first specimen was found.

Grasshopper Sparrow

Ammodramus savannarum

LENGTH:
4-5 in.

WHAT TO LOOK FOR:
short-necked appearance; flat head; short tail; buffy, rather unstreaked breast; streaked back.

HABITAT:
grasslands, meadows, weedy fields, marshes.

The usual song of the Grasshopper Sparrow consists of a few faint ticks followed by a long, dry trill. The bird sounds like a grasshopper. It also eats grasshoppers, and so the name is doubly appropriate. Grasshopper Sparrows nest in colonies in open grasslands, laying eggs in a slight hollow at the base of a short tuft of vegetation. The nest is difficult to find because the female leaves and approaches it on foot, under cover.

Sharp-tailed Sparrow
Ammodramus caudacutus

LENGTH:
4½-5½ in.

WHAT TO LOOK FOR:
gray cheek patch on
bright buffy face; dark
crown; buffy breast with
fine streaking; light
stripes on back.

HABITAT: muskeg, reedy margins of
swamps, marshes.

The Sharp-tailed Sparrow occupies the drier parts of salt marshes; the Seaside Sparrow (*Ammodramus maritima*), grayer than the Sharp-tailed and with just a spot of yellow between eye and bill, prefers the wetter terrain. These species, like many grassland sparrows, are skulkers. A useful technique to bring them up to a visible perch is "spishing"—repeating the sound *spsh* over and over. The trick works with other birds, too.

Vesper Sparrow
Pooecetes gramineus

LENGTH:
5-6 in.

WHAT TO LOOK FOR:
white outer tail feathers; white eye ring; reddish shoulder patch;
brown above, with darker streaks; white below, with brown streaks.

HABITAT:
fields, grasslands with scattered trees, sagebrush areas.

This is a ground-nesting species; it makes a small
depression in the earth and fills it with grasses, roots,
and sometimes hair. The female lays from three to
five eggs, which—if they escape predation—hatch
within two weeks. The young are ready to leave
the nest less than two weeks later. The Vesper Sparrow
often sings its sweet song at dusk—hence its name.

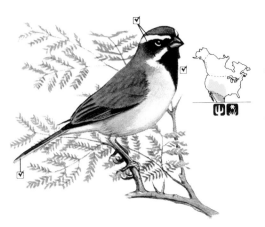

Black-throated Sparrow
Amphispiza bilineata

LENGTH:
4½-5½ in.

WHAT TO LOOK FOR:
black throat; white lines above and below eye patch; plain gray back; white outer tail feathers.

HABITAT:
brushy deserts, semiarid areas.

This species sometimes competes for habitat with the Sage Sparrow (*Amphispiza belli*), but the Black-throated Sparrow is more of a true desert bird and is regularly found far from any water hole or stream. Both have nestlings with pale downy plumage, as do other species that nest in hot, open areas. This coloration is believed to help the young survive, by reflecting rather than absorbing light.

Lark Sparrow
Chondestes grammacus

LENGTH:
5½-6½ in.

WHAT TO LOOK FOR:
facial pattern; clear breast with black spot (immature with streaked breast); tail with white border.

HABITAT:
prairies, open woodlands, fields, farmlands.

Dark-eyed Junco

Junco hyemalis

LENGTH:
5-6½ in.

WHAT TO LOOK FOR:
white outer tail feathers; light pink bill; white belly; rest of plumage slate-gray (with or without white wingbars) or rusty brown with dark head and pinkish-brown flanks.

HABITAT:
coniferous and mixed forests; forest edges and at feeders (winter).

"OREGON JUNCO"
(A WESTERN RACE)

"SLATE-COLORED JUNCO"
(EASTERN RACE)

Until recently, the birds shown above were considered separate species. A third form was the White-winged Junco, found in a limited range in the West. All three are now believed to be races of a single species, and have been "lumped" under the name Dark-eyed Junco. A fourth form, the Gray-headed, common in the Southwest, was recently added to this species.

◀ Lark Sparrow (AT LEFT) Lark Sparrows collect in flocks to feed, but the males are extremely pugnacious near their nests. They fight each other on the ground or in the air, and often these battles turn into free-for-alls. One observer reported seeing five or six males fighting together in midair, "so oblivious to their surroundings that [they] nearly hit me in the face."

American Tree Sparrow

Spizella arborea

5½-6½ in.

reddish cap and eye streak; dark spot in center of pale gray breast.

sub-Arctic areas with stunted trees; brushy areas, grasslands, woodland edges, weedy fields, and at feeders (winter).

Preferring underbrush and shrubs to trees, American Tree Sparrows nest on the ground in dense thickets in the Far North. Whether they appear in large numbers in more southerly regions during winter months depends on the severity of the weather. When the warmth of spring returns, the birds' tinkling song can be heard before they depart for their northern nesting grounds.

Brewer's Sparrow

Spizella breweri

4½-5 in.

finely streaked buffy cap; gray cheek patch; very pale below.

sagebrush, other brushy areas, alpine meadows; weedy fields (winter).

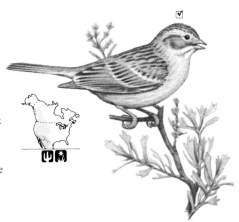

Chipping Sparrow
Spizella passerina

LENGTH:
4½-5½ in.

WHAT TO LOOK FOR:
reddish cap; white
stripe above eye; black
eye streak; pale grayish
below; immature with streaky
brown cap.

HABITAT:
open woodlands, forest edges, farmlands, orchards, suburbs, parks.

IMMATURE

The "Chippy" is named for its song—a trill or string of musical chips, varying from
quite long to very brief. It normally sings from a perch in a tree, often an evergreen.
Evergreens are also favorite nesting sites, although the birds may be found raising young
in orchard trees, in dooryard vines and shrubbery, and occasionally even on the ground.

◀ Brewer's Sparrow (AT LEFT) A shy bird, Brewer's Sparrow tends to keep out of sight, and
its nest is even harder to find. One observer wrote of scaring up an incubating bird;
although it flushed about 3 feet in front of his foot and he saw it leave, he had to get
down on hands and knees and inspect the ground inch by inch in order to discover
the nest. Brewer's Sparrow migrates in flocks with the Clay-colored Sparrow (*Spizella
pallida*), a confusingly similar species with a more eastern range.

MALE

FEMALE

House Sparrow (English Sparrow)

Passer domesticus

LENGTH:
5-6 in.

WHAT TO LOOK FOR:
male with black, whitish, gray, and reddish on head and breast; female brownish above, grayer below.

HABITAT:
farms, suburbs, cities.

Most people regret the efforts made in the 19th century to transplant the House Sparrow from Europe. House Sparrows, which belong to a completely different family from our native sparrows, drive bluebirds, wrens, and other songbirds from nesting sites; they tear up nests, destroy eggs, and toss out nestlings. The species reached its peak early in this century. Since then, numbers have declined, probably because of the scarcity of horses and therefore of the waste horse feed eaten by the birds.

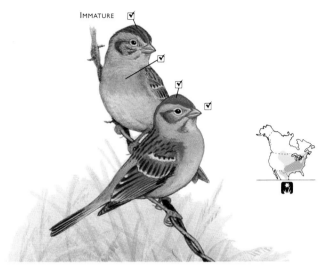

IMMATURE ☑

Field Sparrow
Spizella pusilla

LENGTH:
5-6 in.

WHAT TO LOOK FOR:
pinkish bill, reddish cap; buffy below; immature with
streaked cap and buffy chest band.

HABITAT:
brushy and weedy grasslands, meadows, forest edges.

The sweet song of the Field Sparrow is a series of whistled
notes delivered slowly at first and then accelerated into a rapid
run. In spring, males establish territories by singing and by
chasing their neighbors; once a male is mated, he sings far less
than before. Early in the season, nest sites are on the ground or
only a short distance above it. As the season advances and the
pairs begin second and third families, fewer ground nests are
attempted. Nests, however, are seldom more than 3 feet above
the ground.

Golden-crowned Sparrow
Zonotrichia atricapilla

LENGTH:
6-7 in.

WHAT TO LOOK FOR:
large size; crown yellow, with black border (immature with duller, brown-bordered crown); breast gray.

HABITAT:
Arctic and mountain areas with stunted trees; spruce woodlands, brushy slopes; thickets, scrub areas (winter).

This western sparrow is most often seen during migration or in winter, when it may be common on patios and in gardens. It feeds on seeds, seedlings, buds, and blossoms. This bird is large; the Fox Sparrow (*Passarella iliaca*) and Harris' Sparrow (*Zonotrichia querula*), a black-throated species with a mid-continental range, are the only bigger North American sparrows.

IMMATURE

White-throated Sparrow
Zonotrichia albicollis

LENGTH:
5½-6½ in.

WHAT TO LOOK FOR:
white throat; gray breast; black and white striped crown, often with yellow patch in front of eye (crown of immature with brown and buff stripes).

HABITAT:
woodlands with dense brush; brushy areas, forest edges (migration, winter).

IMMATURE

White-crowned Sparrow

Zonotrichia leucophrys

LENGTH:
5½-7 in.

WHAT TO LOOK FOR:
crown broadly striped with black and white (light and dark brown on immature); gray breast; pink or yellowish bill; pale throat.

HABITAT:
mountain thickets, areas with scattered brush and trees; roadsides, suburbs (winter).

The trim, elegant White-crowned Sparrow breeds in brushy, open terrain, whether in the sub-Arctic, in western mountains, or along the Pacific Coast. The nest site is usually on or near the ground. Male and female approach the nest differently: the male flies in directly; the female lands 10 to 15 feet away, then moves in by stages, pausing often to perch.

◀ White-throated Sparrow (AT LEFT) The White-throat is often nicknamed the Canada Bird or the Peabody Bird, in imitation of a typical song, written as "Oh, sweet Canada, Canada, Canada," or "Poor Sam Peabody, Peabody, Peabody." But there are regional dialects among White-throated Sparrows, as well as marked individual variations. And because the White-throat is abundant and whistles its sweet song loudly and not too fast, these variations are especially noticeable.

Swamp Sparrow
Melospiza georgiana

LENGTH:
4½-5½ in.

WHAT TO LOOK FOR:
reddish cap; gray face and breast; whitish throat; buffy or pale tawny flanks; rusty wings.

HABITAT:
brushy swamps, bogs, marshes; fields, weedy edges (migration, winter).

Within its breeding range this is one of the last diurnal birds to fall silent at night and among the first to tune up in the morning, long before daybreak. Sometimes Swamp Sparrows keep singing through the night. Their musical trilling—richer than the Chipping Sparrow's but otherwise quite similar—sounds from all over the northern marshes where they nest. One authority writes that some swamp sparrow phrases are double. The birds sing two different songs on different pitches at once—"the higher notes being slow and sweet…, and the lower notes faster and somewhat guttural."

Song Sparrow
Melospiza melodia

LENGTH:
5-7 in.

WHAT TO LOOK FOR:
heavily streaked below, with dark central breast spot; longish tail; immature more finely streaked.

HABITAT:
forest edges, brushy areas, thickets, hedgerows, parks, beaches.

IMMATURE

GRAY FORM

RED-BROWN FORM

Fox Sparrow

Passerella iliaca

LENGTH:
6-7¼ in.

WHAT TO LOOK FOR:
large size; rusty tail; brown, red-brown, or gray above; streaked below, with large central spot.

HABITAT:
scrubby trees of sub-Arctic and mountain slopes; forest undergrowth; thickets, farmlands, parks (migration, winter).

The husky Fox Sparrow scratches vigorously for seeds, small fruits, and insects among fallen leaves, jumping forward and back with both feet and spraying litter in all directions. Its summer food is mostly insects and other animals; Audubon reported seeing Fox Sparrows eat tiny shellfish in coastal Newfoundland and Labrador. Its voice is as distinctive as its appearance. The song is a series of rich, often slurred whistles run together in a short "sentence." Indeed, the general impression is that of a conversation.

◀ Song Sparrow (AT LEFT) Ornithologists recognize more than 30 sub-species of the remarkably adaptable Song Sparrow. The birds vary considerably in size, with the largest races 40 percent bigger than the smallest. The color ranges from reddish or dark brown to pale gray. The song typically begins with several regularly spaced notes, followed by a trill, then a jumble of notes. Because Song Sparrows seem to learn the structure of their music from other Song Sparrows, local "dialects" are common. And each Song Sparrow has a variety of private versions; no two individuals sing the same tune.

NONBREEDING MALE

NONBREEDING FEMALE

BREEDING MALE

Lapland Longspur

Calcarius lapponicus

LENGTH:
5½-6½ in.

WHAT TO LOOK FOR:
some plumages with chestnut nape; white outer tail feathers; breeding male with black head, throat, and breast; nonbreeding male with white throat and black breast band; female finely streaked.

HABITAT:
tundra; prairies, meadows, beaches (winter).

The dramatic summer dress of this species is never seen by most people, for the Lapland Longspur nests in the Far North. There, ornithologists have noticed that its breeding activities are remarkably synchronized. Most males start singing at once, most pairs mate at the same time, and most egg laying begins on the same date. Most adults and young also follow a common schedule when they molt before migration.

Snow Bunting

Plectrophenax nivalis

LENGTH:
5½-7 in.

WHAT TO LOOK FOR:
mostly white; breeding male with black on back, wings, and tail; nonbreeding male with reddish brown on head and shoulders; female paler.

HABITAT:
tundra; prairies, meadows, beaches (migration, winter).

BREEDING MALE

NONBREEDING MALE

Chestnut-collared Longspur

Calcarius ornatus

LENGTH:
5½-6½ in.

WHAT TO LOOK FOR:
tail white with black central triangle; breeding male with bold facial pattern, chestnut nape, and black underparts; female and nonbreeding male streaked buffy brown.

HABITAT:
prairies, plains, large fields.

MALE

FEMALE

Loose colonies of Chestnut-collared Longspurs breed in shortgrass prairies or weedy fields. The conspicuous male defends his territory by perching on a stone or weed stalk and by singing in flight. The protectively colored female digs a slight hollow near a grass tuft and lines it, mainly with grass. She alone incubates, but both parents supply the young with food. Though the summer diet includes insects, seeds are the mainstay the rest of the year.

◄ **Snow Bunting** (AT LEFT) The Snowflakes or Snow Birds breed farther north than any other species of songbird. The males arrive on their Arctic breeding grounds by mid-May, three or four weeks earlier than the females. The Eskimos welcome them as harbingers of spring. Snow Buntings nest mainly on rocky terrain, usually building their bulky fur- and feather-lined nests in holes and crannies. In winter they flock along coasts and in open country; they feed on fallen grain in fields and pastures and on weed seeds, as well as on sand fleas and other insects.

Index

Credits and acknowledgments for the original edition of
NORTH AMERICAN WILDLIFE

Staff
Editor: Susan J. Wernert
Art Editor: Richard J. Berenson
Associate Editors: James Dwyer, Sally French
Designers: Ken Chaya, Larissa Lawrynenko
Contributing Editor: Katharine R. O'Hare
Contributing Copy Editor: Patricia M. Godfrey

Consulting Editor
Durward L. Allen
Professor of Wildlife Ecology
Department of Forestry and Natural Resources
Purdue University

Consultants
John Bull
Scientific Associate
Department of Ornithology
American Museum of Natural History

James Doherty
General Curator
New York Zoological Society

G. Stuart Keith
Research Associate
Department of Ornithology
American Museum of Natural History

Allen A. Lindsey
Emeritus Professor of Ecology
Purdue University

Roger Pasquier
Executive Assistant to the President
International Council for Bird Preservation
Smithsonian Institution

E. M. Reilly, Jr.
Senior Scientist in Zoology
New York State Museum

Contributing Artists
Chuck Ripper
Ray Skibinksi
Guy Tudor
John C. Yrizarry